Cork City Libraries
WITHDRAWN
FROM STOCK

SPICE ODYSSEY

Paul Merrett was born on the spice island of Zanzibar amidst a melting pot of cultural influences. During his career he has spent time working in many exotic corners of the world. Paul gained a Michelin star at the London restaurants l'Interlude and The Greenhouse. He now co-owns and cooks at The Victoria near Richmond, winning Best London Gastro Pub at the Great Pub Awards 2011. Paul has appeared regularly on TV. He has presented *The Best*, *Ever Wondered About Food* and *Economy Gastronomy* for the BBC as well as making regular appearances on *Market Kitchen* and *Saturday Kitchen*. He is the author of *Using the Plot* and co-author of *Economy Gastronomy* with Allegra McEvedy. Paul is an ambassador for Compassion in World Farming and Freedom Foods.

PAUL MERRETT

SPICE ODYSSEY

From asafoetida to wasabi,
recipes to really
excite & inspire

Photography Jan Baldwin ❁ Illustrations Anita Mangan

KYLE BOOKS

1835 8140

This book is dedicated to my mum, Delphine Merrett — friend, culinary inspiration and enthusiastic consumer of all things spicy! Thanks Mum...

Published in Great Britain in 2013 by
Kyle Books, an imprint of Kyle Cathie Ltd
67–69 Whitfield Street
London W1T 4HF

general.enquiries@kylebooks.com
www.kylebooks.com

ISBN: 9780857831569
10 9 8 7 6 5 4 3 2 1

Paul Merrett is hereby identified as the author of this work in accordance with section 77 of Copyright, Designs and Patents Act 1988.

All rights reserved. No reproduction, copy or transmission of this publication may be made without written permission. No paragraph of this publication may be reproduced, copied or transmitted, save with written permission or in accordance with the provision of the Copyright Act 1956 (as amended). Any person who does any unauthorised act in relation to this publication may be liable to criminal prosecution and civil damages.

Text © 2013 Paul Merrett
Photography © 2013 Jan Baldwin
Endpapers photograph © Jan Baldwin/Narratives
Spine photograph © 2013 Bernard Zieja
Design © 2013 Kyle Books
Illustrations © 2013 Anita Mangan

Photography: Jan Baldwin
Illustrations: Anita Mangan
Design: Anita Mangan
Prop Styling: Lesley Dilcock
Food Styling: Annie Rigg
Project editor: Sophie Allen
Copy editor: Emma Bastow
Editorial assistant: Tara O'Sullivan
Production: Nic Jones and David Hearn

A CIP record for this title is available from the British Library.

Colour reproduction by Scanhouse

Printed and bound in China by C & C Offset Printing Co. Ltd

Contents

Foreword by Cyrus Todiwala OBE

It is not often that a chef gets the opportunity to write about another chef's book, and, then to top that, for it to be one on a subject they are every bit as passionate about, too.

That Paul Merrett shared my enthusiasm for spices came as a bit of a surprise to me, but it was enough, along with the honour of being asked, for me to blurt out the word, 'Yes!' without hesitation. I have known Paul professionally, of course, for several years, but as I've got to know him more and learnt more about him, and the similarities in our careers, my respect for him has grown. I got to know him for who he is and to appreciate the passion that guides the work he does. Finally, I learnt that the man was born in Zanzibar and naturally grew up amidst spices and the best cloves in the world. This book exudes the word SPICE at every stage and it is a topic very dear to my heart. All my working life in Britain has gone towards raising the profile of spices. I was delighted to be asked to write this foreword.

Paul's writing is humorous, down to earth and from the heart. Finding out about his childhood, amidst the wonderful aromas and smells of a very developed kitchen, involving myriad cultures, shows how these early experiences leave an indelible mark on one's life going ahead. What sheer luck, and what strengths must have been developed at an early age.

A life of fun and excitement develops into a deep love for what one does and Paul's recipes are totally descriptive of that. As I read the recipes, they reminded me of my own childhood, of noisy and strong-smelling bazaars, of a mother who, before her marriage, learnt to cook very little, who was moved from her comfort zone into a large, bustling metropolis, where her own personal style emerged with the help and guidance of seasoned elders, as she developed into a confident cook whose tasty food lingers on for all those that tasted it long after she is gone. She left a legacy in the hands of her son.

Paul makes you want to try his recipes, to work with them and to enhance your own creativity and skills. His honesty shines through here and he tells things as they are. He encourages you to be the judge of your own palate, to use recipes as guidelines and, once accustomed, go forth and conquer with thy own spirit, to mould and change the flavours that suit you best. Advice like this can only be given by a chef who has total confidence in what he is doing.

Reading this book, one gets the feeling of working alongside a great chef, challenging his own senses and recapping dreams of flavours from his childhood. Lucky indeed!

Enjoy, I say, explore, I say, enter with gay abandon, I say and create your own magic.

Pots & pens – an introduction

When I was 16, I opened an envelope and was dutifully informed by the Surrey County Council Education Board that I had failed every exam put before me, and that my life would now spiral out of control as I stared into the face of poverty and vocational underachievement (it didn't say all of that – my parents added some of it). I was actually unconcerned at my dismal exam results. I was young, life was fun and I was upbeat that everything would turn out all right in the end.

The very fact that this is being written as the introduction to a book, with my name on it, may suggest that I was right and that I didn't need those examination results at all but, were it not for my mum, things could have turned out a whole lot worse.

I remember a very uncomfortable conversation where she outlined my job prospects. It wasn't a long conversation! We talked about what I *wanted* to do (play centre-mid for Manchester United, be the next Paul Weller, er, that's it) and then we talked about what I probably *could* do. On the latter list was cooking.

I had always enjoyed eating. I was actually very good at it. I was adventurous and had a big appetite, which suggested that a culinary career of some description might be the answer. As luck would have it, Guildford Technical College had a reasonable catering department and the academic requirements for enrolment were zero – this was looking like my kind of career! As I climbed upon my Lambretta and zoomed off for my first day at college, I may have dreamt that I could make a living from cooking, but I would not have even dared imagine that I might top up this living by writing a cookery book. This is actually book number 2½ (I co-wrote the last one) and I sometimes wonder if medical attention has ever been required within a Guildford bookshop as Paul Merrett's former English teacher collapses, in the cookery department, on seeing the name of such a disappointing student!

Writing a book is always daunting. I should be well used to the process, but I still find myself full of dread and self-doubt. In case you are unaware of how these things are done, I shall explain the process in easy-to-understand stages:

1. Forget the traumas involved with one's previous book.

2. Have an idea around which the new book will be based. It might be Mediterranean cookery, or perhaps family food on a budget, or even spicy food.

3. Visit several publishers and 'hard sell' your idea, claiming that you have the authority and expertise to write said book whilst desperately hoping they don't ask for references and past sales figures.

4. Sign deal, boast to friends and drink beer.

5. Usually the morning after stage 4, wake up and PANIC!

Panic because you suddenly realise that you have signed a contract stating that you will produce a 208-page book full of insightful expert advice (remember that 'hard sell' moment?) and over 80 original, glamorous recipes to boot.

My biggest fear is that no one will buy the book. My first two books sold okay, so I really shouldn't worry, but I still tremble at the thought of the chap across the road proudly telling me that he'd purchased my first book for £2 in a charity shop in Norwich. That really dents an author's ego, you know. As a chef my ego is no less fragile. I have spent a career trying hard to earn accolades and decent reviews to prove my worth as a cook.

A book feels very much like a statement of intent, a self-explained vision of what I stand for as a chef and in as much, this particular book is one, given the opportunity, I was always going to write. Spice has touched my life from very early on. I was born on the spice island of Zanzibar, which is about 30 miles off the coast of Tanzania, East Africa. The island has an incredibly rich cultural heritage. On arrival from the mainland, one can't help but notice

Pots & pens – an introduction

the mishmash of buildings and architecture, the exotic aroma of culturally diverse foods, and indeed the several different shades of people, all of whom make up what is modern day Zanzibar. The reason for such diversity has its historical roots in the dark and shameful past of slavery. In the nineteenth century 50,000 slaves a year passed through Zanzibar city, or Stone Town as it is more commonly known. Zanzibar was also a major port in terms of spices. Arabic and European traders were frequent visitors, and it was not long before they realised that the hot climate with regular rainfall was perfect for spice cultivation. Cumin, cinnamon, cardamom and ginger were all grown successfully, but it was cloves that became Zanzibar's major export.

I was born into this cultural melting pot in 1967, a short while after Zanzibar achieved independence. My mum (a South African with 1960s wanderlust) learned to cook in Zanzibar, and much of what she learned had strong Indian and Persian roots. Even after we made the move back to the UK, she carried on cooking up curries on a regular basis, and her love of spicy food has been a huge influence on my own cooking.

Having graduated from Guildford Technical College, I did what all young chefs should do – I went and worked for as many of the day's great chefs as possible. By doing so I was not only honing my skills, but I was also unknowingly (and inevitably) focusing very much on the culinary style of the day, and back in the 1980s and early 1990s that style was still very much dominated by a European, and particularly French, *haute cuisine* approach to food. Asian food was around, but not thought of in terms of 'fine dining'. It wasn't until I went to work for a brilliant chef called Peter Kromberg that I started to see ingredients

such as coriander, ginger and a range of spices, all familiar to me as a child, being used in modern high-end cuisine, as a result of his own travels as a chef.

When I finally became a head chef I had one purpose in mind. I wanted to win a Michelin star, and I would gladly have given every penny I'd earned for the honour of seeing my name in the red book! As such I once again turned away from more exotic cuisine to pursue a tried-and-tested European formula to achieve my ambition. Once I had achieved the Michelin star I relaxed a little and started to think more about ingredients that I wanted to use, rather than those I thought I should use, and slowly spices started invading my menu, but still in a very low-key way. It took a stern lecture from the finest food journalist of a generation to make me consider my spicy talents more seriously.

One lunchtime the said food journalist, Matthew Fort, popped in to review the restaurant. The kitchen was put on red alert and I was a little concerned that he had ordered, alongside the very French-influenced duck terrine and braised breast of lamb, a dish that I had been playing around with which had very Indian influences – a seared fillet of wild sea bass on top of sag aloo with an onion bhaji and tomato chilli jam. Knowing that a dodgy review can break a chef's reputation, I was worried as I approached his table. He said very nice things about the duck terrine and the lamb, and then he looked me in the eye and said, 'The sea bass, Paul, tell me about the sea bass.' So I hesitantly told him what I've just told you, about Zanzibar and spice influence, and he replied, 'Young man, it was the best dish of all. I suggest you ditch all the French stuff and concentrate on dishes like that.'

If I'd had an ounce of commercial instinct, I would have resigned there and then and pursued his suggestion by opening one of the first restaurants cooking fine-dining Asian food. I didn't, and I've enviously watched many of my contemporaries do just that and do it brilliantly. However, from that day I have incorporated spice within my menus to a much greater effect, to the point where I felt I had a book burning within me. And you've got it in your hands right now!

Things are very different these days. My home city, London, is full of fabulous restaurants from every corner of the globe, fancy-pants expensive establishments as well as many great local ones. Things have changed at a similar pace for the home cook, too. As the world shrinks, spices are taking over. Thanks to the gallant, albeit shady, endeavours of bygone European explorers, spices have been available to the cook for many years. But whereas they were once prohibitively expensive, for the exclusive enjoyment of only society's most wealthy diners, they are now, with a few exceptions, relatively cheap.

Spices are everywhere. From natural remedies, scented candles, perfumes, mulled wine, breakfast cereal and whacky high-street cappuccinos, to the UK's favourite dish, according to recent polls, chicken tikka masala. I hope this book has something for every spicy cook. The beginner need be assured that not all spicy food, by any means, will be mouth-burning hot. Much of the finest spicing is also the most subtle.

This book is a collection of recipes that I enjoy cooking and eating. It dodges between countries and continents with no apology. There are many classic spicy dishes that aren't included and some quirky home-invented ones that are. My only aim is to provoke inspiration and exploration, because those two qualities are always apparent in all of the world's finest cooks.

Open letter to family & friends

Dear family and friends,

This book seemed the perfect opportunity to get something off my chest. Over the years, many of you have enjoyed foreign holidays. When we were younger these tended to be in Europe – Spain, Greece, Turkey, etc. – and as you've all grown fat and wealthy, your holidays have gone more long-haul to places like India, Mexico, Thailand and Vietnam.

Most of you return with small presents, often in exchange for feeding the cat or, as I live six tube stops from Heathrow Airport, for providing free parking. My wife always ends up with something (normally alcoholic) from duty-free, whilst I get the same thing from all of you – a small wicker basket filled with tiny plastic bags of spices. As you hand it over, you tell me about the amazing market and the 100-year-old grey-bearded salesman who explained that these were the finest spices in the world. They are not – frankly, they're crap and you've been conned.

If you want to buy me whole star anise, black cardamoms or cinnamon sticks, go online and buy them from a specialist shop. I guarantee that the small bag of 'top-grade' finely ground saffron is at best turmeric, and probably years old. I'm not being ungrateful, I love your cat and I'd feed it for free, but next summer can I have a decent bottle of gin?

Thank you.

A short note about the recipes

I seldom pick up a cookery book and use *every* ingredient or follow *every* instruction. Cookery writers are sometimes so passionate about *their* way of doing something, they make it seem as if that's the *only* way of doing something. I'm sure I can be just as intimidating, so, to counteract this, here are just a few words of culinary diplomacy...

Nearly every one of the recipes in this book is available for change if you deem fit (that said, some of the desserts are a little more resistant to change). If I suggest using an ingredient that your best friend hates, there is no point in you cooking it for them, so feel free to choose an alternative ingredient in its place. Obviously I think the recipes work just as they are, but I'm keen for you to have a go, whatever the cost!

When it comes to spices, it's very difficult to be spot on every time. Tastes vary from person to person and to this end I have tested these recipes on the taste buds of others, not just on my own, so I hope things are about right. Salt is worth a mention. As a young chef I used lots of the stuff. Since having children and taking more of an interest in such matters, I've cut down dramatically. Moderate amounts of salt do appear in many of these recipes through necessity in terms of flavour. If you wish to omit it, that's fine by me. Where I've used soy or fish sauce I've tended to leave out additional salt.

Finally, measurements are paramount. Great cooks *do* measure things, rather than chucking around estimates with gay abandon. Buy some measuring spoons – you'll be shocked to see that what you thought was a pinch is in fact a teaspoon!

A word about your shopping list ... and an ethical lecture

Ultimately it is your decision on where and how you do your shopping, but I feel a lecture coming on, so here are a few words on food ethics.

MEAT & EGGS

Being an ambassador for the RSPCA's Freedom Food campaign and also Compassion in World Farming, I've spent a good deal of time banging on about the animal welfare standards employed by producers supplying my industry and the wider consumer market. A good cook has respect for his or her ingredients, and I do think it's now fairly easy to find meats of all variety that have been farmed to the highest standard. Years ago, if I had wanted a chicken reared with just a little care and compassion, I would have had to phone up some sandal-wearing hippy in a crofter's cottage. That's no longer the case.

If you are at all unsure, read the labels carefully, talk to your local butcher or accost a supermarket manager. The internet is not only a great source of information (both organisations mentioned above give excellent up-to-the-minute information), but also allows us to buy meat direct from the farmer. Of course farming to such exacting standards costs money, and ultimately you and I, the consumer, pay the extra cost. My suggestion is to eat less meat and, when you do, eat the best meat available. When it comes to eggs, the compromise is zero. Pay the money for free-range, uncaged, barn hens' eggs.

FISH

My Dad is a marine biologist and I can remember him delivering stern and scary teatime lectures on the state of the oceans as far back as the 1970s. The situation remains critical for many species, and unfortunately some of them are our favourite types to eat, so a little experimentation with alternatives is required.

All of the fish used in this book have been listed on the various websites outlining sustainable fish in the UK at the time of writing; however, situations change continuously, so stay up to date with what can be eaten and what is best avoided. Much depends on geography. Species in abundance in one corner of the globe are not necessarily numerous in another, so stay informed.

FRUIT & VEGETABLES

I'm going to neatly duck all the arguments about organic versus non-organic production and simply say that, where possible, buy local and seasonal. Obviously many of the ingredients in a book written around the subject of spice are exotic ones available only in warmer climates, so you may, at times, depending on your hemisphere, need to relax the 'local' stance somewhat!

Right, that's it – no more lectures on what you can or can't do food-wise. It's cooking all the way from here on.

Stocking up

This book is very much intended for those of us who enjoy cooking at home. As such I have tried to avoid calling on (probably expensive) technical equipment that I take for granted in my professional life, but would not dream of buying for my home cooking. The same applies for ingredients. A professional chef has immediate access to just about any ingredient required with the minimum of fuss, whereas in general the home cook must rely on what's available in local shops. That said, it would be impossible to write a decent spicy cookery book without occasionally straying into the unknown, so I thought a few tips on purchasing and storage might encourage the wary novice to give the recipes a go.

I'm certainly not suggesting that anyone should rush out and buy every ingredient all at once – that would be putting way too much faith in a chap who has only written two previous cookery books, and could easily have written a dud – but my endeavours have resulted in a tip or two, so it's worth passing them on.

First off is a quick inspection of your kitchen store cupboard. If yours is anything like mine, it probably contains the vacuum cleaner, a dustpan and brush, the kid's dirty trainers and a plastic bag full of other plastic bags, which you fully intend to reuse one day. Above all this stuff are three shelves, which house all the dry ingredients we use to cook, at home, for family and friends. Towards the front are all the items that get used and replaced on a regular basis – rice, pasta, baked beans, vegetable oil, etc. – and behind this are the jars and bags of bits we buy once, cook with once and keep forever. I bet if you were to take out all those used-only-once-then-forgotten bits, you would find a rather large collection of spices.

Spices are indeed dry and long-lasting – you could put a jar of coriander seeds in a locked vault for a hundred years and, when opened, it would look exactly the same. However, the purpose of spice is not visual, it's aromatic. Spices age within the jar and, as they do, they diminish in flavour dramatically. It's worth pointing out here that whole spices last longer than the ground version of the same spice – more on this on page 15.

Buy small amounts of spice at a time, from a shop that restocks regularly, thus ensuring you are always using the most pungent version. Make sure lids are always put back on properly and find a reason to go back to that spice and use it up whilst it's still on top form. A good, witty, imaginative spice cookery book is an absolute essential to achieving this end – this one, perhaps! As you work your way through your spice collection, keep the emptied jars handy, because your enthusiasm for spicy food will lead you to make up rubs and mixes of your own, which you can then store in these recycled jars – ingenious, thrifty and environmentally friendly!

The recipes here also call for bottled sauces of various types to be dripped, tipped and stirred in, and again many of these may be lurking in your cupboard, as they are in mine. I have, in fact, got such a vast array of exotic Asian bottled sauces in my store cupboard that I know I will never get round to using them all up. Last night I encouraged my less than charming child to taste some soy sauce that was two years out of date. This morning they were still alive and well at breakfast time, so I had some too and found it to taste exactly as I recall it tasting two years ago, thus leading me to suspect that ready-made bottled sauces have a much longer aromatic life than spices.

And so to shopping. The supermarket is the obvious place to start. Most of us live very close to a supermarket (my wife sometimes seems to live in the supermarket, and has certainly spent enough to buy a medium-sized one of her own), so upon deciding on a recipe to cook I expect most people will walk along the spice aisle, hoping that what they require is available. My own local supermarket is quite good, but only quite. No asafoetida, or whole mace, or brown mustard seeds, or fenugreek. The answer is the internet. There are lots of fabulous online spice shops run by enthusiastic types who have roamed the globe looking for the very best and most exotic spices. Most divide their spices by country or region, meaning you will be able to experiment with the same spice from different parts of the world. You will also find interesting spice mixtures such as baharat or laksa spice, which certainly aren't available in my supermarket. I'm not going to point you to any particular site, but there plenty and most are excellent. Try a search engine, but be carefully when typing in the words 'hot, spicy and exotic'...

Local ethnic markets are great for sourcing spices. I live very close to Southall, an area of London with a large Asian community, where the shops are bursting with fabulous collections of dried spices and fresh ingredients, many of which I've never seen elsewhere. If you're off on holiday, it's well worth visiting the local food markets and seeing what's available. I could easily spend an entire two-week vacation at the Istanbul spice market! One tip, though: many of the markets sell their spices from wonderful carved wooden bowls without any indication as to what the brightly coloured contents actually are. Ask for names and write them down, because if you don't, that very spice will end up hidden forever, at the back of your store cupboard, above the smelly trainers and the recycled shopping bags!

Tools of the trade

First of all, don't worry, I'm not trying to sell you anything here. As yet there is no Paul Merrett Kitchen range. (I'm not averse to the idea – it's just that nobody's asked me yet. If you're a kitchen utensil manufacturer and your budget's medium-to-large, give my agent a call.) The following recipes make use of various utensils and equipment. Some you will already own, but there may be a few items that you'd like to add to your Christmas list.

PESTLE & MORTAR

This really is an essential piece of kit for preparing the dishes in this book, or any spicy cookery book. The recipes often call for dried spices and fresh herbs to be ground and pounded before use. There are many types of pestle and mortar available, but avoid fancy-looking porcelain or glass ones as they are way too fragile, whilst attractively-carved wooden ones are too lightweight. Instead go for a heavy-duty granite or marble version. The mortar is the bowl-shaped bit and it's important to get the right size. If the bowl is too small, you will not have room to work the ingredients, meaning you will need to grind in stages, which is a pain. On the other hand, if the mortar is too wide, you will always be chasing stray unpounded bits around the bowl. I think the optimum bowl size for a domestic kitchen is 10–15cm.

Because you will be pounding and grinding a huge variety of ingredients, many of which will be highly flavoured spices, it's a good idea to keep the pestle and mortar as clean as possible. An old trick that works very well is grinding raw rice, as it lifts off all traces of flavour from both the pestle and the mortar.

ELECTRONIC SCALES

Buy a set that goes down to at least 1g. Weighing spices is important and, because they are such pungent ingredients, a missed or extra gram here or there can make or break a dish.

DIGITAL TIMER

Essential. At the restaurant every section has a timer. Buy a magnetic one and stick it on the hood of the stove.

DIGITAL PROBE

My mum would say, 'I'm not Heston Blumenthal, dear, I don't need a digital probe.' No Mum, you're not, and that's why you *do* need one! They are very useful for working out if a slab of red meat is cooked to your liking. As a rough guide, meat cooked to an internal temperature of 50°C will be rare, 55°C will be medium-rare, 60°C will be medium and 70°C+ will be dry and horrible, or well done, as some call it . Obviously poultry and the like should be cooked to the higher temperature to ensure safe eating.

FLAT HOT PLATE

This flat, cast-iron plate can be heated to a very high temperature for the searing of fish, shellfish and some meat. Sometimes the hot plate has two sides, one of which is ribbed (see Griddle Plate, below).

GRIDDLE PLATE

Similar to a flat hot plate, a griddle plate is a ribbed cast-iron plate that will leave 'bar marks' on whatever you're cooking. Good for creating the chargrilled look or for cooking marinated ingredients that could stick to a conventional pan.

MANDOLIN

If this is going on your Christmas list, it's important that the purchaser does not confuse it with the small guitar of the same name. The best (and happily the cheapest) mandolins are the plastic Japanese types, which come with various blades. Using a mandolin is fraught with danger – use the guard provided!

THERMOMETER

At various points in the book a little deep-frying occurs. You may own a proper fryer with a thermostat, but most of us just grab a pan and pour in a little vegetable oil. A thermometer will allow you to regulate the temperature. As a guide, successful frying will take place at 170–180°C.

MEASURING SPOONS

Very useful when working with spices. This book, and every other one on the subject, will direct you to use a teaspoon of this and a tablespoon of that. They're cheap and cheerful, so make sure you own a set.

Using whole spices

Generally speaking, I prefer to buy whole spices and grind them myself when required. Spices keep much better whole than powdered. That said, not all spices are easy to find in their raw state so it's better to buy small amounts of spice powders regularly than large amounts in one go. For once, bulk purchase does not save money!

I know a little bit about wine and even less about perfume, but experts in both fields talk about 'notes' when discussing flavour and aromas. Spices, widely used in scents and perfumes, of course, can also be discussed in this way. Many whole spices have intricate layers of flavour or aroma rather than just one consistent 'note'. The trick for the cook is to release as many of these as possible. Grinding a whole spice has this effect immediately. The finer the spice is ground, the more the aroma is exposed and therefore released. This is particularly important when preparing a fast-cooking dish.

Heat also releases a spice's aromas. At a chemical level these aromas are termed 'volatile', which to you and me (cutting out a whole load of probably very necessary science!) means that as they are heated the aromas evaporate and leap out of the spice, allowing us to detect them. This is why most spices are added early on in the cooking process. The very best time to introduce the spice is when you are frying onions and garlic at a high heat in oil. It's also the reason behind dry-frying the spices. First, let's just clarify that term. When one dry-fries a spice, no oil is added to the pan. The spice, or mixture of spices, is cooked in the hot pan alone, allowing these volatile oils to do their thing. The slight colouration, or 'toasting', of the spice adds another dimension yet again. The spice is generally, though not always, cooled and then ground to a powder before being used.

I think the simplest demonstration of the pungency of a whole spice versus a powdered version of the same origin is to take two small spoons of vanilla ice cream. Sprinkle pre-ground nutmeg onto one and on the other finely grate a similar amount of whole nutmeg. The results speak for themselves.

The dishes within this section are all fairly quick and simple to prepare. With my restaurant-chef head on, I would call them all starters, but that feels way too restrictive. Many of them would make a fantastic lunch, a light supper or even a mid-afternoon snack, so please don't feel that you can only make them if you have a further two courses to serve afterwards! In fact, most of the Asian-style food I have eaten has been a succession of smaller dishes with no beginning, middle or end to speak of, and I think that's definitely the most exhilarating way of serving and eating food.

Starters, snacks & carefree grazing

66 Blessed are the cheese makers …

Whilst churning 2 litres of sheep's milk into a lump of Pecorino is beyond the skill (and frankly patience) of most of us, you can now add 'cheese maker' to your family crest with this most basic of cheese preparations. Labneh is a popular dish all over the Eastern Mediterranean and throughout the Middle East, and in every deli in Notting Hill too, come to think of it!

Labneh is made by simply hanging Greek yogurt in a muslin bag to filter out the whey. It's often served just on its own with pitta bread, but I like to add a little spicy sumac and a bit of sweet fruit. Sumac is a flowering plant common in Africa. The berries of the plant are ground to a powder and used as a spice – they are very slightly citrus-flavoured, with a great crimson colour, perfect to sprinkle over the pure white labneh. 99

Homemade labneh with sumac, pomegranate & basil

SERVES 8 AS A STARTER OR AS PART OF A LUNCH SPREAD

450g Greek yogurt
¼ teaspoon salt
1 teaspoon sumac
1 pomegranate
a few small basil leaves
1 tablespoon extra-virgin olive oil
warm pitta bread, to serve

You will also need a large square of
   clean muslin.

Line a deep bowl with a sheet of clean muslin. In a separate bowl, stir the yogurt and salt together. Pour the salted yogurt into the muslin cloth and tie the excess muslin with string so that the yogurt is contained within it. Hang the muslin bag over a bowl – if your fridge has racking rather than glass shelves, this should be easy; however, if, like me, you didn't consider labneh production when buying your fridge, I suggest you tie the muslin bag to a wooden spoon and balance the spoon over a bowl (nifty, eh?).

Leave to drain for at least 24 hours (I occasionally give it a little squeeze of encouragement) or until much of the liquid has drained out and the remaining yogurt in the muslin is thick and fairly dry but still creamy.

It's worth noting that people are not given their own plate of labneh – they barge, stretch and jostle to get their share. Spoon the labneh into the centre of a serving plate and use the back of a spoon to spread it out into a circle. Sprinkle a generous line of sumac right across the plate.

Cut the pomegranate in half and remove the seeds, then scatter these randomly over the labneh. Dot about the basil leaves, drizzle over the olive oil and serve with warm pitta bread.

" The wonderful thing about the internet is the lightning speed at which the ignorant can be transformed into the informed. Three minutes ago I knew that the betel leaf was a green leaf from some sort of creeping, vine-like plant found in Asia. Four clicks later and I'm a betel leaf expert of some standing, and feel confident enough to inform you that betel leaf is often chewed and consumed for its mildly psycho-stimulating hallucinogenic properties, it's mentioned in the *Kama Sutra*, it can stain one's teeth horribly if chewed extensively, and… hang on, should this ingredient be in my book? Anyway, you should be able to find betel leaves in your nearest Asian supermarket.

I recently spent time cooking on a beautiful Thai island where betel leaf was served as a kind of snack before a meal (think Twiglets). It was really fun assembling the little leafy parcels, making them as sweet, fiery-hot or citrusy-sharp as desired. My teeth did not get stained at all, my libido remained unaffected and I didn't suddenly feel the urge to pen a rock opera, so I reckoned this recipe was okay to send to the publisher. The dish is a sort of help-yourself starter, with everyone making the betel leaf wraps at the table, so your job is more about assembling the ingredients and less about spending ages in the kitchen. "

Betel leaf wraps with ginger, crispy shallots, chilli & broken cashew nuts

SERVES 4 AS A SMALL PRE-MEAL SNACK

40g fresh ginger,
  peeled and finely diced

2 red bird's eye chillies,
  finely sliced into rings

3 tablespoons Crispy Shallots
  (see page 186)

2 tablespoons unsalted cashew nuts,
  broken up a little

1 lime, finely diced, skin and all

3 tablespoons finely chopped
  fresh coconut

8 betel leaves

FOR THE SAUCE

1 small red onion, finely diced

40g fresh ginger,
  peeled and finely diced

4 tablespoons palm sugar

juice of 1 lime

4 teaspoons fish sauce

1 tablespoon soy sauce

From the ingredients list there is only item that needs cooking – the sauce.

Put all of the ingredients for the sauce into a pan and bring to a simmer. Cook until reduced by half the original volume – the warm consistency of the sauce will resemble sweet chilli sauce (as it cools it may 'jam-up' a little more, which is fine). Chill until you are ready to serve.

Pile the remaining ingredients onto a large tray or chopping board, and serve with the sauce.

Now, your friends may be well-travelled, worldly-wise types, in which case you can rely on them knowing what to do with this array of odd ingredients. However, just in case they are in need of guidance, it's important that you know what advice to give, so …

Take a betel leaf and pinch one side slightly to make a very shallow cone shape. Put a small amount of each ingredient into the cone and top with a little of the sauce. Fold over the excess leaf to close the parcel up, open wide and shove it in! I have found that taking a small polite bite from the parcel nearly always results in all the ingredients arranging themselves down the front of my shirt, so frankly I suggest going for the all-in-one approach, but it's up to you.

CORK COUNTY LIBRARY

66 People presume that, because I am a chef, my children are somehow genetically programmed to enjoy all types of culinary delights, including those from the vegetable patch. Well, it's not true! I have suffered the same dramas as most parents in getting my pesky kids to eat 'one a day', let alone five. For a long time I considered only three methods of persuasion:

1. Bribery. Eat your greens and I will give you pudding. This does work, but also means making industrial amounts of puddings.

2. Threat of punishment. If you don't eat your greens, I will drop a brick on your iPad. I like this option, but my wife, a primary school teacher, says it's negative and counter-productive.

3. Fear. If you don't eat your greens, all your hair will drop out, your skin will go scaly and your teeth will go brown. This method stopped working when one child pointed out that this was a near-perfect description of Grandpa and he does, in fact, enjoy vegetables.

It was my (annoyingly) sensible wife who suggested a fourth option – make vegetables taste very nice! So herewith my children's favourite vegetable dish. Okay, it does involve frying, so it's not a perfect everyday choice, but as an occasional snack it's a big hit.

I tend to use long-stemmed broccoli. I think the stem is the best bit and should never be wasted, particularly if you grow your own. What the crunchy battered broccoli really needs is a clean-tasting yogurt dip. This one is based on the sort you get with your poppadoms in an Indian restaurant and is so versatile – I make gallons and use it with loads of different things. Anything cooked quickly in a tempura batter is best done at the last minute, so it's important to have everything ready, including serving dishes and dip, before you start cooking. 99

Ginger beer-battered broccoli tempura with minted mango yogurt dipping sauce

SERVES 4 AS A STARTER OR TRENDY SNACK!

250g tempura flour

450ml ginger beer, chilled

2 litres vegetable oil, for frying

300g tenderstem broccoli

FOR THE YOGURT DIP

500g Greek yogurt

100g mango chutney

25g mint sauce (ready-made is fine)

We will start with the dip. Empty your yogurt into a large bowl and stir in the mango chutney and mint sauce. If the chutney contains large pieces of mango, you may wish to chop it up a little before stirring in. Right, the dip is done! (By the way, this will make plenty, so chill what's left over and buy some poppadoms.)

Tip the flour into a mixing bowl and pour on the ginger beer whilst gently whisking. Don't over-whisk the batter: a few small lumps will merely make it seem more authentic and crunchy.

Pour the oil into a large, heavy-based casserole pot and heat to 170°C. (If you don't own a thermometer, I'd advise asking for one this Christmas, but as a very rustic alternative you could check the temperature by dropping in a small piece of white bread. If it fizzes and goes a golden-brown colour, you are good to go.) Dip the broccoli into the batter one stem at a time, turning to make sure each stem is well coated. Allow any excess batter to drip off before carefully placing the broccoli into the hot oil. Allow to fizz for a few seconds before gently stirring the oil to make sure the broccoli stems do not stick together. When golden-brown, carefully remove the broccoli using a slotted spoon and drain on kitchen paper. Serve immediately alongside the dip.

66 Italy is not a country that immediately springs to mind when discussing spicy food. Chopped chilli turns up on the occasional pizza and chilli oil is sometimes used to dress a salad, but it's not standard issue. So this dish is already very slightly brave with its use of fresh, fiery green peppercorns, but the really clever thing is that they are balanced with chilled sweet melon. Fresh green peppercorns are not always too easy to find, though Asian supermarkets do often have them. If you can't get them, look for a tin of green peppercorns in brine.

Now I should confess that I was not clever enough to think up this perfect combination all by myself! I was served this risotto at a tiny restaurant half way up a mountain whilst visiting Le Marche in Central Eastern Italy. The risotto was served after the starter as a prelude to the main course – a course called *primo piatto* in Italian. We hadn't ordered it; it just arrived! It was one of those occasions when you approach a meal with no high expectations at all (I was simply very hungry), and leave the table very slightly humbled by the sheer brilliance of what you have just been served. 99

Fennel risotto with chilled melon & green peppercorns

SERVES 4 AS A STARTER (OR DOUBLE UP FOR A MAIN COURSE)

¼ really ripe orange-fleshed melon, such as Cantaloupe or Charentais

150g unsalted butter, roughly diced

1 small onion, finely chopped

2 garlic cloves, finely chopped

sprig of thyme, leaves only

½ fennel bulb, very finely diced

150g risotto rice (Arborio, Baldo, or my favourite, Carnaroli)

425ml hot vegetable stock (it's fine by me to use a stock cube!)

30g fresh green peppercorns

good pinch of salt

1 tablespoon freshly grated Parmesan cheese

The very first thing to do is peel the melon and cut the flesh into 1cm cubes, then stick it in a bowl in the fridge until just before serving – the melon needs to be really cold when added to the risotto as this gives a wonderful heat contrast.

Melt the butter in a heavy-based saucepan and chuck in the onion, garlic, thyme leaves and fennel. Cook gently until the vegetables are slightly softened and 'fizzing' in the butter, but not coloured at all. Add the rice, stir and cook for around 2 minutes (it's important to control the temperature so that the rice and vegetables do not colour).

Add the stock, a ladleful at a time – it needs to be added bit by bit and you must stir continuously. Stirring is an important manoeuvre for the risotto maker because it causes the rice grains to rub and release starch, and this means you will end up with a good, creamy risotto.

I reckon you will need most if not all of the stock. However, after 15–18 minutes of adding, stirring and simmering, taste the risotto and if you are happy with the texture, it's time to move on to the final stage.

Reduce the heat to the bare minimum and stir in the peppercorns and salt. Make sure all risotto eaters are sitting down ready for their meal, then stir in the Parmesan and finally the chilled melon. A rocket and red onion salad dressed with extra-virgin olive oil would be great with this if serving as a main course.

" A traditional Andalucían gazpacho is, of course, a chilled soup made using tomatoes as a base along with other vegetables and herbs found in that part of the world. It's a fine soup and in no need of any customisation or modernisation by me or any other food writer. However, unless there is some obscure EU law that I've not been made aware of, I am allowed to steal the word gazpacho and use it to describe my own chilled soup.

Watermelon is a funny old fruit. I don't much care for a wedge of watermelon (or a fake rolex watch, if you're that 'salesman' on the beach), but used in a salad with salty feta, perhaps, or in a soup such as this gazpacho, it works very well. We tend to think of gazpacho as a soup eaten at the beginning of a meal; however, in Spanish bars it is often served from a jug as a drink, which is how I recommend serving my version. Make up a batch of watermelon gazpacho and serve it in frozen shot glasses (perhaps with a sneaky slug of vodka!) either before your meal or on the side with a spicy dish. The gazpacho is best served as fresh as possible, but do leave enough time to chill it thoroughly in the fridge. If you are going to serve this in glasses, pop them in the freezer before you get going so they are super-cold and frosty-looking when required. "

Watermelon, mint & chilli gazpacho

MAKES ENOUGH TO FILL 16 SHOT GLASSES

750g chunk peeled watermelon

1 beef tomato

20 mint leaves

20g fresh ginger, peeled and chopped

2 red chillies, chopped

Remove as many pips as you can from the watermelon and roughly dice the flesh. Chuck it into a bowl, then roughly dice the tomato and add to the watermelon. Add the mint leaves, ginger and chillies.

Now all that remains is to convert your bowl of prepped ingredients into a liquid. I think this is best done in a food-processor rather than a blender as a food-processor will leave a little texture, which is nice, whilst a blender will blitz everything to a super-smooth consistency (as is a blender's purpose in life – I'm not complaining, just saying!). So tip your ingredients into a food-processor and whizz to a fairly smooth but still textured soup.

Have a taste – you should pick out the watermelon as the overriding flavour, but there should be just a hint of acidity from the tomato, a background minty note and of course a slight smack of chilli. Apologies if I sound like a West End sommelier describing a wine that's going to cost you a month's wages. If more mint or chilli is required, pound a little more in a pestle and mortar and stir through the gazpacho.

Chill the gazpacho in the fridge until really cold, then decant into shot glasses and serve.

66 You may have already guessed that this is no winter warmer! This soup is best served icy cold on a very hot day. Never vice versa. In terms of saucepans and stove tops, the soup involves no real cooking at all. However, applying heat to a soup is very important in terms of extracting maximum flavour, so for one like this, with no cooking as such, the challenge is to get the full-on flavour of the totally raw ingredients. Very fresh, ripe ingredients and a blender are key to our strategy! I recommend making the soup 24 hours in advance, if you can – this will allow the flavours to mingle and develop. Once it's made, store it in the fridge in an airtight container. 99

Cucumber, avocado & yogurt soup with fresh peach, ginger & fennel seeds

SERVES 6

pinch of fennel seeds

75g fresh ginger, peeled

1 avocado, peeled, stoned
    and roughly chopped

1 cucumber, peeled
    and roughly chopped

2 very ripe peaches, stoned and
    roughly chopped

100g Greek yogurt

juice of ½ lime

5 mint leaves, roughly torn

1 ripe plum tomato, roughly chopped

1 teaspoon sumac

250ml water

200ml coconut milk

½ teaspoon salt

FOR THE ADDITIONAL BITS

2 red chillies, finely diced

½ cucumber, finely diced

1 sweet, ripe peach, stoned and
    finely diced

1 tablespoon fennel seeds, ground

12 mint leaves, thinly sliced

2 teaspoons sumac

This soup makes a fantastic starter on a balmy evening – you could even serve it in shot glasses alongside another spicy starter. I've split the ingredients into two sections – the first is for the soup itself and the second is for all the bits that are stirred into the soup just before serving. A great way to serve the soup is with the additional bits in bowls to let people customise their own soup.

To make the soup, grind the fennel seeds to a powder in a pestle and mortar and set aside. Grate the ginger and then press it through a sieve over a bowl to extract as much juice as possible. Keep the juice and chuck away the pulp. Put the fennel seeds and ginger into a blender and add all the remaining soup ingredients (I just about manage to get all this done in one batch in my blender, but if yours seems a little small, it's fine to do it in a couple of batches). Blend until smooth and then pour the soup into a container and shove it in the fridge.

Just before serving prepare all the 'additional bits' and either stir them into the soup (if you don't trust your family and friends to share fairly!) or put them in bowls on the table so that people can add as much or as little of each as they wish.

A few years ago my son was asked at school what his favourite food in the whole wide world was, and he replied, 'My Mum's pea soup.' When I was told this by his teacher I obliged by laughing, as expected, and saying something like, 'Yes, well it is very good', before going home and smashing his PlayStation with a mallet. I wasn't only upset because he had chosen something Mum made instead of me – I can forgive a child that young for ignoring my culinary endorsement by countless food critics (including Michelin). No, it wasn't just that. I was upset because actually Mum's pea soup isn't that great to start with. She doesn't season her soup, she puts in way too much potato and she cooks it for so long that it ends up a sort of khaki colour. This pea soup is in another league, I guarantee. But I'm not bitter and it's all forgotten now…

This recipe is for 1.5kg of yellow split peas – freeze what you don't need in freezer bags (I put 2 servings per bag). I make most of my soups in larger quantities than required so that I can have a ready supply of soup at all times. Unfortunately so does my wife. I should also say that this soup could easily be made with dried lentils of any colour in place of the dried peas.

Spiced yellow split pea soup

MAKES AT LEAST 20 PORTIONS

100ml vegetable oil

1 onion, finely chopped

3 garlic cloves, finely chopped

5cm piece of fresh ginger, peeled and grated

1 beef tomato, roughly chopped

2 celery sticks, roughly chopped

1 medium carrot, roughly chopped

3 teaspoons ground cumin

2 teaspoons chilli flakes

2 teaspoons garam masala

1½ teaspoons ground coriander

2 teaspoons fennel seeds

seeds from 5 cardamom pods

20g salt

1.5kg dried yellow split peas

chopped fresh coriander, to serve (optional)

Heat the oil in a large casserole pot (the dried peas will swell during cooking – as will lentils, if you're using them – so make sure you use a decent-sized pot). Chuck in the onion, garlic and ginger and fry gently until slightly coloured for 3–4 minutes. Add the tomato, celery and carrot and stir everything together for half a minute. Tip in the remaining ingredients except the dried peas and fresh coriander, stir and leave everything to sizzle away for a minute or so.

Add the dried peas (I never soak them prior to soup production, by the way) along with 5 litres water and bring to a simmer. Cook for 35 minutes or until the peas are swollen and soft – the kitchen should smell good, too.

You now need to blend the soup to the desired consistency. I like my soup to have plenty of texture, so I use a stick blender, which I randomly plunge in and blend until I get the desired effect. You can enjoy your soup just as it is; however, if you have your son's teacher round for lunch you may like to go the extra mile and stir in some chopped fresh coriander before serving.

I had this soup in a roadside café in the middle of nowhere in rural Arizona. It's very quick and easy, and if this were a glossy magazine, it would definitely be called Store Cupboard Soup. Editors of food magazines and producers of daytime TV cookery shows are desperately keen on food that can be produced without any shopping involved! Egg in a soup is not unusual – I've discovered poached eggs floating in all manner of soups in the past – but a fried egg is less common. I'm imagining that there is a Spanish, or more likely Mexican, influence going on here, though it was actually served to me by a Native American.

Don't skip the fried bread – it's the ingredient that pulls everything together – and make sure you serve the yolk very runny and deliver advice on breaking the egg up within the soup before eating it. Finally, for any food magazine editors or daytime TV producers browsing this tome, I'm very happy to rename the soup 'No Stop-to-Shop Soup' if it gets this book a spot of free marketing.

Fried egg soup with smoked paprika & ground chilli

SERVES 4

3 tablespoons olive oil

2 garlic cloves, crushed to a paste

2 plum tomatoes, finely diced

1 teaspoon smoked paprika

pinch of salt

½ teaspoon chilli flakes, ground to a powder

700ml chicken stock (homemade would be fantastic, but if you've got a cube in that store cupboard…)

4 slices of bread from a white bloomer

4 free-range eggs

3 spring onions, green parts only, thinly sliced

Heat 1 tablespoon of the olive oil in large pan and fry the garlic for 1 minute until very slightly browned. Add the tomatoes and simmer for about 2 minutes until softened and much of the juice has reduced. Stir in the paprika, salt and ground chilli flakes. Pour in the stock and bring to a simmer, then leave the soup to cook while you get on with the next bit.

Heat another tablespoon of the olive oil in a frying pan and fry the slices of bread on both sides until golden and crispy. Tear them in half and put a half into each serving bowl. The other halves will be served on the side.

Add the remaining olive oil to the frying pan and fry the eggs until slightly under-cooked (they will continue cooking in the hot soup). Put a fried egg into each bowl on top of fried bread, and pour over the hot soup. Sprinkle with the spring onions and serve.

66 This book sets out to inform, inspire and entertain in equal measure. Occasionally I may even dare to be controversial, but I have no wish to provoke a major international diplomatic incident, so I need to make it clear right here and now that this soup could be from Vietnam, the Philippines, Thailand, China or even Cambodia. I'm not issuing it a passport; I'm just hoping you may cook it up and give it a try. As recipe titles go, this one is textbook-perfect. It contains seafood, it's spicy hot and soured with lime juice. What I love about this soup is the purity of flavour – it feels cleansing. The soup should be made just before serving and if you taste it at its various stages, you will notice the layers of flavour as they build up.

Now this recipe is more of a list of suggestions than a set of rules. I firmly believe that chicken stock works better as a base stock for this soup than (the possibly more obvious) fish stock. You are welcome to experiment. Whichever you choose will present you with your next decision… do you make a fresh stock or go with a shop-bought cube? I go for the compromise solution. I simmer 1.2 litres of stock made with a cube and chuck in 6 chicken wings to give it a bit of body. Chicken wings are dead cheap at the butcher's. After simmering the wings for 20 minutes I fish them out and give them to the cat – I keep the stock. Right, so your stock is simmering and your guests are ready to eat; now begins the hot and then the souring process.

Another decision concerns the king prawns. To get maximum flavour from the prawns you must cook them whole, unpeeled, heads and all. Let your guests peel them or, do as I do, eat everything bar the head, which you can chuck in the bin. If your guests are the timid type, it's probably worth peeling them. It's your call. 99

Hot & sour seafood broth

ENOUGH TO CLEANSE 4 SOULS

1.2 litres chicken stock (see intro)

6 chicken wings (optional)

2–3 red bird's eye chillies

8 kaffir lime leaves

2 lemongrass stalks, each cut into 3

30g fresh ginger, peeled

60g palm sugar

8 shiitake mushrooms, sliced

1 raw squid tube, sliced into rings

8 raw king prawns in the shell

splash of fish sauce

juice of 2 limes

20g fresh coriander, very roughly chopped

Make up the stock using my suggestion above, or as you see fit, and bring to a simmer in a large pan. Pound 2 of the chillies with the lime leaves, lemongrass and ginger in a pestle and mortar. Don't pound to a paste, but bash it up well. Tip into the simmering stock and stir.

Add the palm sugar – if it's in cake form, grate it into the stock; if it's a liquid, simply spoon it in. Taste the broth (as it is now known) – it should have a punch from the chillies but you should also pick out a sweetness from the sugar as well as lots of flavour from the ginger, lemongrass and lime leaves. Don't expect any sourness, as we haven't done that bit yet! So… here's another decision: if you think the broth could be hotter, bash the third chilli and chuck it in. My view is that this soup needs to be fiery hot but you can overrule that if you like, as I'll never know!

Right, back at the stove… chuck in the sliced shiitake mushrooms, squid rings and prawns – they will all be cooked and ready in 4 minutes, so crack on. Add a splash (that's about 2 teaspoons to the pedant) of fish sauce to give a slightly musty, oriental flavour – and it negates the need for any salt, by the way – and add the lime juice. Stir in the coriander and have a taste. Is it spicy? Sweet? Aromatic? Sour? Good, that's ticked all the boxes. Ladle it into soup bowls, making sure everyone gets equal amounts of prawns, squid and mushrooms.

Last Tuesday one of my staff cleared out the chest freezer. As a stand-alone fact, this may not impress you that much. Perhaps you have a good knowledge of food safety and hygiene and you were presuming that we should be cleaning our freezer every Tuesday as a matter of course, which I assure you we do... I merely mention it in passing, because it led to a culinary discovery of epic proportions.

Part of the job of cleaning the freezer is to compile a list of any bits found lurking for which there appears to be no obvious use. These are the bits that make a chef his money. Find useless bits, create a dish, give it a French name, double the price and *voilà*! A business plan is born. On the list last Tuesday was 2kg of prawn shells. They weren't labelled raw or cooked, which would have been helpful. However, as they were a dull grey as opposed to a pinky-orange colour (foolishly called 'Lobster-red' by a certain paint company – foolish because we all know that lobsters are a beautiful blue-black colour), we knew that they must have been the shells of raw king prawns, peeled and served on a previous menu.

One of my chefs suggested that we use them to make the classic French soup, bisque. I was all for this. (French name...double the price – are you thinking what I'm thinking...?) Bisque is a rich shellfish soup often thickened with rice. Traditionally the shellfish used, be they prawn, crab or lobster, are inferior specimens which would not sell at the market, or indeed the shells of said shellfish, such as those found in our freezer. So I commissioned a bisque to be made with our prawn shells, at which point one of my other chefs said that it might be a good idea to veer away from the classic French recipe, and instead use coconut milk as the stock and infuse a little chilli and lemongrass for extra flavour. I love to see that sort of inspirational creativity springing from the mind of one of my chefs. Better still, when it happens in private so that I can claim the inspirational idea as my own, but unfortunately on this occasion the idea was witnessed and shared by all those gathered around the now neatly stacked and labelled freezer.

I am not a man who considers himself a fusionist guru simply through adding lemongrass and chilli to a classic French dish – that kind of innovation is lazy and often results in a clash of culture and flavour. However, sometimes it just works, so I give you Prawn & Coconut Bisque.

Prawn & coconut bisque

SERVES 6 GENEROUSLY

75ml olive oil

1kg prawn shells (see note below)

½ fennel bulb, roughly diced

1 carrot, roughly chopped

1 tomato, cut into 8 wedges

½ onion, roughly chopped

4 garlic cloves, roughly chopped

pinch of saffron

1 star anise

30g risotto rice

3 x 400g tins of coconut milk

600–850ml water

1 heaped teaspoon salt

3 red bird's eye chillies

4 lemongrass stalks

75g fresh ginger, peeled

15 lime leaves

First up, heat the olive oil in a large casserole pot over a high heat. Tip in the prawn shells and cook fiercely for about 3 minutes or until they take on a pinkish colour and give off a lightly roasted aroma. Reduce the heat and add the fennel, carrot, tomato, onion and garlic. Fry gently for 2 minutes, then add the saffron, star anise and rice.

Pour in the coconut milk and 600ml of the water and bring to a simmer. Cook for 30 minutes or until the rice grains are soft and swollen. Tip the soup, shells and all, into a blender and whizz until smooth.

Strain the soup to remove any fibrous bits and then return to the pan. At this point you should have a rich-tasting shellfish soup with a creamy coconut flavour lurking in the background. If you feel it is a little thick, add some or all of the remaining water. Add the salt in stages and taste as you go.

Heat the soup back to a simmer. Bash the chillies, lemongrass, ginger and lime leaves in a pestle and mortar and add to the soup, stirring well. Simmer for 2 minutes and only then remove from the heat and leave to cool. This short simmering with the chilli, lemongrass, ginger and lime leaf keeps the fresh flavour of these aromas alive, whilst the slow cooling ensures maximum infusion. Reheat the soup and serve with chargrilled naan bread or store in the fridge or freezer to enjoy later.

A SHORT NOTE ON OBTAINING PRAWN SHELLS

The easiest way to lay your hands on prawn shells is to buy whole, fresh, unprepared king prawns and choose a dish that requires peeled prawns. (You won't believe this, but such a dish can be found – King Prawn Pappardelle with Chilli, Lemon, Garlic, Basil & Parsley on page 122. You may need to eat this dish more than once in order to obtain 1kg shells, but that's no hardship, believe me.)

Once you have peeled the raw prawns, wrap up the shells and stuff them in the freezer. If you are the type that goes in for a bit of high-end cookery, you may, from time to time, end up with crab or lobster shells. Keep these, too, because bisque can be made from a variety of shells, both cooked and raw.

The title may contain two words that you are not that familiar with, so I shall explain. Tilapia are fish native to East Africa, and are farmed extensively in Northern Europe, among other places. They are herbivorous fish, which in ethical terms is a good thing, and they taste great, which in culinary terms is also a good thing. They are perfect to use for an escabeche, but that's no help to you yet, because I haven't explained what that is…

An escabeche is a dish made with fried fish, which is then marinated in a sweet-and-sour liquor. It has been around for many years, turning up in English cookery books as far back as the seventeenth century. It's thought to have Spanish origins, but many cuisines have a similar dish. I guess originally the purpose of the sweet-and-sour liquor was as a preservative.

So, now we are all up to speed, I need to tell you a story. I started my career at the Ritz Hotel in London during the 'last hurrah' of nouvelle cuisine. Food had to be delicate and very, very pretty. I spent hours pouring aspic jellies over carefully cut vegetables and shaping seahorses out of puff pastry. I learned a lot, but it was my next job which changed everything for me. I went to work at Le Soufflé restaurant near London's Hyde Park Corner for a chef called Peter Kromberg. He was a born leader and a fantastic cook. All these years later I am certain that he was the greatest influence on me, my career and my approach to cooking. He taught me to taste food, he mocked my efforts at fancy plates and encouraged me to compromise prettiness at the expense of flavour. This is his escabeche recipe, and it proves a point – it has a huge flavour!

Tilapia escabeche

SERVES 6

5 tablespoons olive oil

250g tilapia fillet

½ small fennel bulb, cut into
   very fine strips

1 large carrot, cut into very fine strips
   (us chef types call this julienne)

1 onion, thinly sliced

1 garlic clove, finely chopped

2 tablespoons white wine or
   cider vinegar

150ml water

2 sprigs of fresh thyme

2 tablespoons chopped fresh coriander

pinch of ground coriander

2 star anise, halved

small pinch of saffron

pinch of cayenne pepper

2 teaspoons caster sugar

pinch of salt and twist of pepper

lettuce leaves, to serve

The first thing to do is fry the fish. Heat 1 tablespoon of the oil in a hot frying pan and add the fish, skin-side down. Fry for 2 minutes or until the skin has coloured a little. Transfer the fish to an earthenware dish, laying it skin-side down, and set aside at room temperature. (The fish will not be cooked through at this point. The rest of the 'cooking' process happens when it comes into contact with the pickling vegetables.)

Heat the remaining oil in a pan and chuck in the fennel, carrot, onion and garlic. Cook for 3 minutes or until softened but not coloured. Pour in the vinegar and water and bring to the boil.

Add all of the remaining ingredients except for the lettuce leaves and stir for 30 seconds. Remove the pan from the heat and spoon the mixture over the fish – make sure you get a good even spread of all the bits and liquid. Cover the dish with clingfilm and puncture a few holes in the top. Leave to cool at room temperature, then transfer to the fridge and leave well alone for 24 hours.

Before eating your escabeche, take it out of the fridge at least 1 hour before serving, to let things warm up slightly. Place the tilapia onto a serving plate and put a small pile of the vegetables on top. Trickle over some of the juice from the dish and serve at room temperature with a few lettuce leaves.

" This is a quirky yet useful recipe. Quirky because cakes should be sweet and made with fruit or chocolate and definitely cream, not stuffed full of olives, spices and cheese; useful because it is a really quick, simple and tasty alternative to homemade bread. You can knock this up in under an hour minus all the hassle of bread making. It's great served warm with unsalted butter, just as you would a fresh loaf of bread, or serve it with sliced charcuterie or a smoked fish pâté, or topped with a salad of beetroot, watercress and goat's cheese. "

Savoury cheese & olive cake with chilli & smoked paprika

MAKES 1 LOAF

4 free-range eggs

150ml dry white wine

150ml olive oil

250g plain flour

1 teaspoon baking powder

1 teaspoon smoked paprika

pinch of chilli flakes

pinch of salt

180g pitted green olives, drained and each one sliced into 3 rings

110g sun-blushed tomatoes, drained if very oily

140g mature Cheddar, grated (any hard cheese would work)

I usually knock this up in an electric food mixer but the process is exactly the same and almost as quick by hand.

Mix the eggs, wine and oil – the beater attachment of the mixer is best, or use a wooden spoon if making by hand. Tip in the flour, baking powder, smoked paprika, chilli flakes and salt and again beat the mixture enough to incorporate everything.

Fold in the olives, tomatoes and grated cheese by hand. Bake in a lined loaf tin at 170°C/gas mark 3½ for 45 minutes. Allow to cool in the tin for 10 minutes and then turn out onto a wire rack for a further 10 minutes to cool.

Serve whilst fresh and warm or store in an airtight container for up to 3 days and warm gently before serving.

66 Everyone loves crispy filo prawns, right? But how often have you been offered homemade ones? Well, the reason for that is they are, admittedly, a tiny bit fiddly to make, but don't let that put you off trying your hand at them. The good news is that they can be made well ahead of time when you've got a quiet and empty kitchen available.

White radish is sometimes called mooli or daikon, but it's the same thing and fairly widely available in most supermarkets. It's important to tell you that the world's heaviest daikon weighed over 30kg. That's a whopper, and luckily you don't require one that big. 99

Crispy filo tiger prawns with white radish & soy chilli dipping sauce

MAKES 12 WRAPPED PRAWNS, IDEAL FOR 4

1 small white radish

2 carrots

270g filo pastry

12 raw peeled tiger prawns

2 red chillies, thinly sliced

1 tablespoon coarsely chopped fresh coriander

1 free-range egg, beaten, mixed with 2 tablespoons cold water

vegetable oil, for frying

FOR THE SOY CHILLI DIPPING SAUCE

1 tablespoon sweet chilli sauce

1 tablespoon soy sauce

good pinch of chilli flakes

juice of 1 lime

1 tablespoon sesame oil

FILO PASTRY OBSERVATIONS

The first thing to note is that filo pastry is a tricky customer. Shop around and experiment until you find the brand that works best for you. Once you've opened the packet of filo, you should lay all the sheets on a tray, cover the top sheet with a cloth and store it in the fridge. Use the filo, sheet by sheet, straight from the fridge.

But before we even open the packet of filo we must cut the vegetables. Cut the white radish and carrot into strips the same length as the tiger prawns, about 1mm thick and 5mm wide. A mandolin is a great tool for this job, but other than that it's down to your knife skills!

Cut a strip from a sheet of filo about 10cm long and 3cm wider than the prawns. Lay a prawn at one end of the filo strip (it's worth making a small incision in the curved back of each prawn so that you can push the prawn flat) and arrange a small pile each of the white radish, carrot, chilli and coriander alongside the prawn.

Lightly brush the exposed filo with the beaten egg and water, fold the excess over either end of the prawn and then roll up until the prawn and vegetables are encased. Wrap all the prawns in this way and either cook straight away or store them on non-stick greaseproof paper in the fridge for up to 3 hours, if you wish.

To make the dipping sauce, simply mix the ingredients together in a bowl.

Heat some vegetable oil in a large, deep frying pan – the level of the oil should be deep enough to allow the prawns to float. Cook the prawns, in batches if needed, turning a couple of times, until golden brown and crispy on all sides. Remove using a slotted spoon and drain on kitchen paper for a few seconds before transferring to a plate. Serve with the dipping sauce.

There's just so much to tell you about this dish. First, we need to discuss the term 'potted', which refers to a method of food preservation popular in medieval times. The pot was actually a heavy, flour-based, inedible pie case made specifically for holding food, rather than for eating.

Many types of food – such as eels, lampreys, pigeon, pork and countless other delicacies – were cooked and then decanted into these pie crusts along with melted butter. Once the butter had set and the pie was sealed, the food within would last much longer, allowing for transportation. Over time the pie case was replaced by a dish or pot, but with very much the same purpose.

Brown shrimps were stored this way. They would have been processed and potted where they were caught, which would probably have been Morecambe Bay in Lancashire, an area long associated with the small brown shrimp (or *Crangon crangon*, in case any marine biologists are tuned in) used in potted shrimps. Mace and nutmeg were commonly used 'back then' as flavourings, and for me the spicy butter is one of the most appealing parts of the whole dish, particularly when balanced with the liveliness of dill and the sharpness of lemon.

I love this dish. We serve it in the restaurant on toast (not in a pot) and that is how I'm going to suggest you make it. If you want to put the mixture into a pot, that's fine by me (do so at the point where I suggest getting your clingfilm out); however, I think this way actually makes life easier.

I should have mentioned above, but forgot in all the excitement of my history lesson, to tip you off about brown shrimp purchasing. Raw brown shrimps have a brown shell, but if you're buying cooked and peeled ones, they will be a dusky pink colour. Don't confuse them with the Norwegian type used in a prawn cocktail – brown shrimps are much smaller. If you ask your fishmonger, he should definitely be able to get hold of them.

English potted brown shrimps with nutmeg & mace

SERVES 4 AS A GENEROUS STARTER OR LIGHT LUNCH

250g cooked and peeled
   brown shrimps

about 20 ice cubes

600ml cold water

125g unsalted butter

1 shallot, finely chopped

pinch of sea salt flakes

1 heaped tablespoon chopped
   fresh dill

grated zest of 1 and juice of ½ lemon

generous pinch each of ground mace,
   cayenne pepper and grated
   nutmeg

the best wholemeal granary bloomer
   you can find

watercress salad, to serve

Tip the shrimps into a large glass or metal bowl, then tip the ice cubes into an even larger bowl and pour over the cold water (if you don't have a bowl large enough to hold the ice cubes and water, improvise – use a large pan, or the washing-up bowl, or even the kitchen sink). Place the bowl containing the shrimps into the iced-water bowl.

Put the butter, shallot and salt into a pan over a low heat and gently melt the butter (on no account should you allow it to burn or colour). Remove from the heat and leave to cool for 3 minutes, then pour the melted butter mixture over the shrimps.

Stir gently using a spoon or spatula as the ice cools the butter, which will eventually harden and set. It's important to keep everything moving so that the butter sets evenly rather than against the cold edges of the bowl. Whilst stirring, add the dill, lemon zest and juice, mace, cayenne pepper and nutmeg. Keep stirring until the mixture loses its liquidity and starts to thicken.

Get your clingfilm out! Lay a sheet of clingfilm about 50cm long on the work surface. Spoon the shrimp and butter mixture onto the clingfilm and use your hands to work it into a large sausage shape around 6–8cm in diameter. Roll the shrimps up in the clingfilm and tie at either end. Chill in the fridge. Your prawn 'sausage' will need at least 3 hours in the fridge to set completely.

Do whatever you like during this time – it's no business of mine ...

When you are ready to serve, turn on your grill, cut 4 slices from the bloomer and toast them on both sides. Remove the shrimp 'sausage' from the clingfilm and cut into 4 generous slices about 3cm thick. Place 1 slice onto each piece of toast and squidge them a bit to cover the toast evenly. Place the toasts back under the grill until the butter just begins to melt. Don't leave for too long – 2 minutes should do it. Serve immediately with a watercress salad.

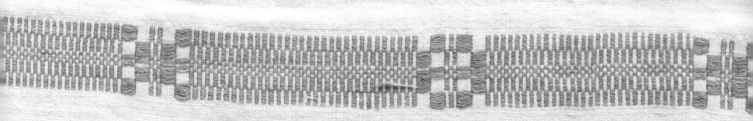

"Scallops are certainly not a cheap meal option. Furthermore, the best scallops (for eating, and for the environment) are hand-dived, which are unfortunately more expensive still. So this dish is one you'll probably make infrequently and save for when you are entertaining friends, rather than sitting in front of the telly with a tray on your lap! I first tried this in Thailand and loved the purity of it. Simple flavours merely 'upselling' the key ingredient.

The freshest scallops are those sold in the shell, meaning they could well still be alive when you buy them. I have given a free tutorial on opening a scallop shell just in case it seems a little daunting. If scallops are not your thing, or you struggle to find any really nice ones, you could use thinly sliced sea bass or even salmon.

A quick word about the tomatoes. If you are the type of person who dashes around the supermarket at a hundred miles an hour paying little or no attention to what us chefs call 'considered sourcing', hold on. Really ripe, sweet, red tomatoes are key to this dish. Rummage through what's on offer and select the very best available. The tomato water is best made a day in advance, if possible."

OPENING SCALLOPS IN THE SHELL

A scallop is a bi-valve, meaning it has two shells. The upper shell is fairly flat whilst the lower shell is concave and holds the meat. Always store scallops in the shell with the flat shell uppermost. As scallops are an expensive ingredient, you want to extract as much of the meat as possible and a palette knife is the best tool for the job. Lay the scallop on a work surface with the flat shell uppermost. Carefully work the palette knife inside the crack between the two shells and run it across the inside of the flat shell, ensuring the knife stays flush with the top shell, releasing it entirely.

You will now be eyeball to eyeball with a scallop. The meat we want is the large white muscle. Scoop the palette knife under this muscle to release it completely.

The shells can be thrown away or given to friends as ashtrays (they will be really pleased!).

Gently pull the orange coral away from the scallop – you can pan-fry the corals and have them as a cook's treat for lunch tomorrow. You are now left with the large white meaty scallop and some frilly gunky nonsense that we call 'the skirt'. Pull away the skirt and discard it. *Voilà*, one glorious scallop. Once you've prepped all of your scallops they can sit happily in a container in the fridge for a few hours.

Raw diver scallops with tomato water, fresh ginger & lemongrass

SERVES 4

8 large diver-caught scallops, removed from the shell (see opposite)

1 avocado, peeled, stoned and diced into 1 cm cubes

½ cucumber, halved, deseeded and diced into 1cm cubes

a few small lettuce leaves, such as frisée lettuce, lamb's lettuce, and fancy cresses

20 salted peanuts

pinch of chilli flakes

1 tablespoon caster sugar

1 tablespoon Crispy Shallots (see page 186, or buy ready-made from Asian supermarkets)

FOR THE TOMATO WATER

6 really ripe plum tomatoes

4 lemongrass stalks

50g fresh ginger

2 red bird's eye chillies, finely chopped

1 tablespoon caster sugar

½ teaspoon salt

A large square of clean muslin is very useful

Right, now to the actual dish. The first thing to make is the tomato water – I would do this the day before if possible. Bring a pan of water to the boil and have a bowl of cold water close by. Remove the eye from the tomatoes (the eye is where the stalk joins) and plunge the tomatoes into the boiling water for 10 seconds. Carefully remove them from the boiling water using a slotted spoon and plunge them into the cold water to halt the cooking process. Peel away the skins and discard, then roughly chop the tomato flesh and throw it into a bowl. Blanching the tomatoes in this way helps to increase the resulting yield of tomato juice.

Cut each lemongrass stalk into 3 lengths and bash with a rolling pin, then chuck into the bowl with the tomato flesh. Grate the ginger (don't bother peeling it) and chuck that in the bowl as well. Add the chillies and stir in 1 tablespoon of the caster sugar and the salt. Now tip everything in the bowl into a blender or food-processor and whizz it all up for about 30 seconds.

Place a large square of muslin in a clean bowl and tip in the whizzed-up pulp. Tie up the muslin and let it hang over the bowl to drip until all the tomato water has come through – a couple of hours. I do this in the fridge. Every now and then give the muslin bag an encouraging squeeze. This should produce about 500ml of tomato water, which you should then chill.

To serve the dish, take your scallops, slice each one into 4 discs and arrange on four serving plates. I usually go for a simple line of scallops, each one slightly overlapping the next. Dot the cubes of avocado and cucumber randomly across the plates, and do the same with the salad leaves.

Bash the peanuts, chilli flakes, caster sugar and Crispy Shallots in a pestle and mortar until they resemble coarse breadcrumbs. Serve the scallops with a bowl of crunchy shallot and peanut crumb on the table for people to add themselves. Finally pour your pungent tomato water into a jug and ask your butler to pour a little over each person's scallops.

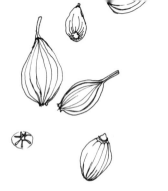

If there were a Crispy Squid Eating World Championship, I would be remortgaging my house and putting all my money on my son, Richie, to come home with the gold medal. Crispy squid is one of those snacks that translates into any language. Spanish, Italian, Greek, Thai, Indian, Chinese...they all have a version. Some years ago I was stationed on the crispy squid section of a buffet catering for some incredibly posh guests at a well-to-do private garden party. Towards the end of lunch a lady in a stupidly large hat glided past my station and told me that the food had been divine (I hate that word as a culinary description), apart from the onion rings, which were chewy and tasted peculiar. I just smiled and thought to myself, if I were Billy Bragg, I'd write that into a song!

The key to frying squid is to have the oil nice and hot, so the squid cooks very quickly. A hand-held thermometer is useful to indicate the temperature of the oil, but remember the temperature will continue to rise if the oil is left on the stove! The usual way of frying squid is to first coat it in either a batter or a seasoned flour. Batter is great but quite messy, so I opt for the simpler seasoned flour approach.

Salt & pepper squid with papaya, chilli & coriander salsa

SERVES 8 AS A STARTER OR 4 FOR LUNCH

350g plain flour

2 tablespoons smoked paprika

1 tablespoon salt

2 tablespoons cracked black pepper

vegetable oil, for frying

12 raw squid tubes, cleaned and cut into 2cm rings, and tentacles (see opposite)

FOR THE SALSA

1 papaya, finely diced

1 small red onion, finely chopped

1 small red pepper, deseeded and finely diced

1 red chilli, finely diced

grated zest and juice of 1 lime

10 mint leaves, finely chopped

20g bunch fresh coriander, finely shredded (stalks and all)

20g fresh ginger, grated

2 tablespoons sweet chilli sauce

2 tablespoons olive oil

First make the salsa. Mix all of the ingredients and leave to stand at room temperature for 1 hour (not you, the salsa!).

Meanwhile, mix the flour with the paprika, salt and pepper on a large plate or dish. Pour the oil into a deep-fat fryer or large pan deep enough to hold 10cm oil. Bear in mind that it will fizz up when you chuck the squid in, so allow for this and don't overfill the pan. Heat the oil to 180°C.

The squid should be floured just before it's fried, so just before the oil reaches the required temperature, toss the squid thoroughly in the seasoned flour and shake to remove any excess. Working in small, manageable batches rather than hoofing the lot in all at once, gently slide the squid into the hot oil and let fry for about 4 minutes or until lightly coloured. Cooking too much at once will cause the oil temperature to drop considerably, which in turn means that the squid takes longer to cook and therefore ends up chewy, so cooking in batches is really important here.

Carefully remove the crispy squid from the oil using a slotted spoon, drain on kitchen paper and serve immediately with the salsa.

A NOTE ON BUYING AND CHOPPING SQUID

On page 12 you will find a short piece of advice on maintaining an ethical approach to purchasing fish – this applies to squid too, so have a read. Most of us choose our friends based on emotional attachment; however, if you're honest, you may have collected a couple of friends based on good old practical grounds. Some people befriend a mechanic, or an electrician. Plumbers have loads of friends, and some very clever foodie types make sure that their local fishmonger loves them just enough to be of great value when they are buying fish. Fresh fish is always best, and if you can befriend your fishmonger, he will always tell you what is seasonal and fresh, rather than selling you what he might have to chuck out the next day (it happens). You may even be able to develop your relationship to a point where you can call the fishmonger up, tell him what you'd like

to cook and he'll pick it up from his suppliers. He may well ask what size you'd like. Ask for squid with a body of about 15–20cm long – that will give you a decent-sized squid ring.

There's no point in chatting up a fishmonger and then not putting it to good use, so I'd ask him (yes, yes, or her) to prep the stuff. Ask them to give you skinned and cleaned squid tubes (the main body) and also the tentacles. As a starter portion I would work on 1½ tubes per person, and a few bonus tentacles. Before frying your squid place the tubes on a chopping board and, using a sharp knife, cut them into rings about 2cm wide. There are various shapes you can cut squid into before frying, but for this chunky dip I suggest rings are best because you can squeeze and hold the salsa in the squid ring. Clever, eh?

A word on chillies & which to buy for each recipe

ABBREVIATED HISTORY

Records show that, in Mexico, wild chillies were being gathered and eaten by 8,400BCC (before Christopher Columbus). The Spaniards and Portuguese took them to India and South East Asia, and from there they travelled to the Middle East. By the sixteenth century chillies were being enjoyed throughout Europe.

TYPES OF CHILLI

Cayenne, habanero, jalapeño, scotch bonnet, naga, tabasco and bird's eye are just a few of the many types of chillies. Which varieties are available to you will depend very much on where your cooking takes place geographically. When writing this book I had originally decided to be very chilli-specific, but my local selection of supermarkets tend to stock just two varieties, so I decided to stick with what's most readily available:

1. The standard red and green chilli (variety unspecified) is about 7–10cm long with smooth skin. These chillies are flavoursome but never mind-blowingly hot, so I've tended to use them in recipes that require a good visual presence or in dishes that are more subtly spiced.

2. Bird's eye chillies, both red and green, are used in many of the recipes. They are much smaller than our standard friends above, about 3–5cm long, and the skin is slightly wrinkled. The bird's eye chilli is not to be underestimated – it punches well above its weight in terms of spiciness.

Chillies are always hot and spicy; this is the result of years of natural selection. The fiery kick of the cunning old chilli will deter any animal from returning for a second bite … apart from one animal, that is. For some reason humans quite enjoy chomping on really hot chillies, and farmers throughout time have cross-fertilised and genetically selected their seed crop to produce ever more hot and fiery ones. Various studies and much research have been done by biologists, psychologists and inebriated young men eating in Indian restaurants into how much chilli can be consumed, and indeed why we enjoy the sensation in the first place. Though not conclusive, the 'benign masochism' theory seems to be the popular explanation, meaning that we enjoy the thrill of the chilli burn because we know that ultimately it can do us no harm. If this book represents your first steps into the world of spicy cuisine, exercise a little caution. All of the recipes that use chilli work well as far as my taste buds are concerned, but feel free to cut down the quantity if you feel I may be further down the road to culinary masochism than you.

In the early twentieth century a pharmacist called Wilbur Scoville devised a sort of chilli league table. Each variety was assessed and awarded 'heat units' to show which were the hottest of all. The table has had various league leaders as chilli growers cross-breed in search of ever hotter varieties. One little trick worth noting is this – the hottest part of the chilli is the white membrane, or placenta, that attaches the seeds to the flesh. By removing this membrane you will reduce the net impact of the chilli substantially. It's a good trick where you require the visual abundance of chilli minus the total heat. I often finish a dish with a salad of fresh coriander, toasted coconut and red chilli sliced finely on an angle. I remove the seeds and membrane from the chillies so that I can use more chilli for a greater visual impact.

Cooking with chillies can also be hazardous. Chopping boards should be scrubbed well after chilli preparation, otherwise whatever you chop next will be exposed to the juice of the chilli. Always wash your hands thoroughly after chopping chillies and refrain from rubbing your eyes, your nose or indeed any other body part that could be sensitive to the sting of chilli. A good cook should, of course, refrain from any type of bodily rubbing (of themselves or anyone else) until the apron is off and they've left the kitchen, but that's just good old health and safety.

OK, I admit this is a bit of a fancy-pants-restaurant-dish, but hang in there – it's really not difficult to make at all and is guaranteed to lift your culinary status amongst your friends! A ceviche is a South American style of preparing and 'cooking' raw fish in a citrus marinade. No real cooking actually takes place, but the acidity in the marinade breaks down the protein and gives the fish a just-cooked appearance.

And so to the fish itself. Sea trout are the migratory form of our native brown trout that have left the river and swum out to sea, rather than the cross between a trout and a salmon of popular misconception. Feeding out at sea means that these trout can reach a fair size (up to 13kg) so you should have little trouble finding a chunky fillet. The key to success with this dish is the quality of the fish – I use a wild or organic farmed sea trout, and most fishmongers should be able to get a similar fish of similar quality.

The vanilla may seem like a wacky addition, but give it a go. The natural oiliness of the fish balances perfectly with the richness of the vanilla and the sharpness of the lime. Personally I would serve this as a starter but you could double up and make it a main course if you felt so inclined.

Sea trout ceviche with lime & vanilla dressing, lotus root crisps & soya beans

SERVES 4

500g skinless sea trout
½ tablespoon salt
½ tablespoon caster sugar

FOR THE LIME & VANILLA DRESSING
grated zest and juice of 2 limes
1 teaspoon wasabi paste
good pinch of sea salt flakes
2 vanilla pods
150ml extra-virgin olive oil

FOR THE LOTUS ROOT CRISPS
& SOYA BEANS
approximately 40 frozen soya beans
1 lotus root bulb
250ml vegetable oil

TO SERVE
kejap manis (see page 75)
salad leaves or cress (optional)

PREPARING THE SEA TROUT

If at all possible, buy your sea trout on the day you intend to eat it to ensure it is as fresh as possible. Lay the sea trout fillet in a large dish and sprinkle over the salt and sugar. Chill the fish in the fridge for 2 hours, during which time it will release a little moisture. This process, known to intelligent types as osmosis, will change the texture of the salmon very slightly, making it both easier to slice and more pleasing to eat. After 2 hours, wipe the top of the fish with a clean cloth to remove any excess moisture, salt and sugar.

Now, using a very sharp knife cut the sea trout across the fillet into 5mm slices. You should end up with at least 20 slices. Lay the salmon onto 4 serving plates, cover with clingfilm and refrigerate for at least 2–3 hours.

MAKING THE DRESSING

The dressing can be made a good few hours, or even a day, in advance and chilled until needed. Simply whisk well shortly before using. Put the lime zest and juice into a bowl and whisk in the wasabi paste and sea salt flakes. Split both vanilla pods and scrape the seeds into the bowl. Add the olive oil and whisk again to incorporate thoroughly.

THE SOYA BEANS

If using podded soya beans, all you need to do is defrost them before use. If you are using beans still in their pods, defrost a few about 10 minutes before and then pop out the required number of beans.

THE LOTUS ROOT CRISPS

The lotus root crisps can be prepared up to 4 hours in advance. Take the lotus root bulb and slice very finely – this is definitely a job for your Japanese mandolin!

Heat the oil in a small high-sided pan until it reaches 170°C and then tip in the lotus root. Allow it to fizz away until golden brown and crispy. Remove from the oil using a slotted spoon and drain on some kitchen paper. Store in a dry place until needed (and don't forget to take the pot of oil off the heat!). Finally tip a little of the kejap manis into a small bowl and have a teaspoon handy.

SERVING UP

When you are ready to serve up, remove the plates of sliced salmon from the fridge and unwrap the clingfilm. Give the dressing a final whisk, then paint it generously over the salmon using a pastry brush, reserving a little of the dressing. Dot the soya beans over the salmon and top with the lotus root crisps – I like to lay the crisps against each other so that they stand up. Drizzle the reserved dressing around the salmon. Lastly dip the tip of a teaspoon into the kejap manis and allow it to drip over the salmon – don't add too much! If you wish, you can add a small salad leaf or a sprinkling of cress to finish the dish.

WASABI

A number of years ago, I had a Japanese student come to work as part of my kitchen team for a few months. She went home over Christmas and on her return to the UK she knocked on the office door and told me she had brought me a special gift back from Japan. I was very excited, thinking it would be some incredibly expensive high-tech electronic gadget bought in Tokyo, and was a little bemused when I noticed that the gift had been wrapped in damp tissue paper. It turned out to be fresh wasabi, a root grown in water. Most of us will struggle to find fresh wasabi, but luckily it can be bought as a paste or as a powder to which water can be added. It's often called Japanese horseradish. A botanist would point out that it's not a relation of horseradish at all, but the cook would counter that by telling the botanist that the flavour does indeed resemble horseradish. Most people's wasabi education probably begins in a sushi bar where it's offered as a simple paste alongside raw fish, but it can also be used in sauces, pickles, marinades and dressings.

66 This is one of my favourite recipes in the entire book. First, I think it's fabulous to eat, which is obviously a basic requirement when creating a dish, but I also like its purity – clean, healthy flavours with more than a passing nod to Japanese cuisine. We often put this on the menu at The Victoria and it always proves an immensely popular starter. I also make it at home. It's not really a Tuesday evening supper dish as it requires a little more effort than I can be bothered with on a weekday evening, but when friends come over it makes the perfect starter.

This dish also goes some way to demonstrating how I create a recipe in the first place. Shamefully I have had very few original ideas at all. Some chefs just seem able to start the creative process from scratch, which I admire greatly, but that's not me. I'm a plagiariser. Interpreter more than thief, I hope. I see an idea in another chef's restaurant, hijack it and then set about tearing it apart and rebuilding it to a point where I think I can claim custody.

Some years ago I had the great fortune to be sent to New York with someone else's credit card. Result! I was booked to do a few cookery demonstrations each day, but by night I was free to roam the Big Apple in search of culinary excellence. Along with a good friend and fellow chef, I headed off to many of New York's finest ~~strip clubs~~ culinary establishments and ate some terrific food. On the last night, after a foodie conversation with an in-the-know New York concierge, we were encouraged to try out Jean-Georges Vongerichten's latest restaurant at that time, Spice Market, situated in the Meat Packing District. It was the best meal of the trip for me, by far. I've returned to the restaurant several times since and always leave thinking that this could well be my favourite restaurant in the world. The décor is exotic: high ceilings, low tables, cool lighting and lots of carved wood (all of which remind me of Zanzibar in many ways), with great New York service, and the food is sensational.

On that first occasion we were served a dish of finely sliced, very fresh raw salmon, and on one part of the plate was a spicy, crispy onion 'crumb' which we sprinkled over the salmon. There was also a sweet and sharp pickly thing on the plate which I can't quite recall, but the dish was stunning. I knew right then that I was going to use it as inspiration for one of my own back home, and here is that dish. 99

Salmon 'sashimi' with shallot & chilli crunch & pickled cucumber

SERVES 4

450g skinless salmon fillet

2 teaspoons salt

2 teaspoons caster sugar

43g tube wasabi paste

5 tablespoons Shallot Crunch (see page 186)

1 batch Asian Cucumber Pickle (see page 189)

12 Lotus Root Crisps (see page 50–51)

12 tablespoons kejap manis

First 'cure' the salmon using the salt and sugar to withdraw moisture, leaving the flesh of the fish slightly firmer with a meaty texture, and also making it a little easier to work with. Scientific types call this process osmosis. Place the salmon on a large plate or dish, skin-side down (or where the skin once was, because I told you to remove it – just testing!). Mix the salt and sugar together and sprinkle evenly over the salmon piece. Cover with clingfilm and chill in the fridge for at least 3 hours.

Remove the salmon from the fridge and wipe it with a piece of kitchen paper or a clean, damp cloth to remove the excess salt and sugar. Transfer the salmon to a chopping board. The piece of salmon is bigger than the

CONTINUED... ⟶

Salmon 'sashimi' with shallot & chilli crunch & pickled cucumber

CONTINUED FROM PAGE 53

4 portions required, so we can trim the fillet to get a really good shape, which is so important in Japanese cookery. Remove a strip of salmon about 3cm wide from the thinnest side of the fillet, which will leave you with a narrower fillet but of a more even depth. Stick the trimming in the freezer and use it to make fish cakes next week, or give it to the cat.

Find the wasabi and a brush and paint the top of the fillet of salmon with a generous spread of wasabi paste. Pour the Shallot Crunch into a large dish and lay the salmon, wasabi-painted-side down, on top of the shallots. The wasabi will help 'glue' the Shallot Crunch to the salmon. Turn the salmon over and place on a clean chopping board. You should now be looking at a large chunk of salmon with an even spread of crunchy shallots over the top, forming a thin crust.

Using a sharp straight-bladed knife, cut slices about 4mm thick across the salmon fillet. Lay the slices onto 4 serving plates, add a good dollop of the Asian Cucumber Pickle to each slice and top with a Lotus Root Crisp. Drizzle a little kejap manis over each plate using the tip of a teaspoon and serve immediately.

AN APOLOGY

I get frustrated when a cookery writer keeps referring to recipes on other pages, making what seemed like a simple recipe much harder and more complicated. I've tried to limit that manoeuvre in this book in case it upsets you too, but this dish has caught me out. Both the Asian Cucumber Pickle and the Shallot Crunch can be made well in advance.

A NOTE ON SALMON

Not all salmon is the same. For a start, there is wild salmon and farmed salmon. Wild salmon tastes fantastic but is scarce and expensive, so I tend to use a farmed variety.

Look for salmon from a named farm. Most supermarkets and fishmongers will stock a top-end farmed salmon, and often it's organic, but not always. As we are essentially serving raw fish here, freshness is paramount. Don't use frozen salmon for this dish. When buying your salmon, ask for a piece from the head end of the fillet, as the flesh there is thicker and more suitable for this recipe. Ask for the skin to be removed, too. Finally, take care when handling the salmon – if the flesh tears in any way, it will ruin the look of the finished dish.

66 I have a speech reserved for family visits to our local Chinese restaurant. I won't bore you with the full 18-minute version, but it begins, 'Of course kids, this isn't real Chinese food. Oh no. If we were in China we'd be eating...' and then I come out with a list of ingredients which sound like Hannibal Lecter's shopping list, in order to demonstrate how un-Chinese our experience actually is. The truth is I've no idea, because I've never actually been to China. My kids invariably inform me that they couldn't give a damn how Chinese the restaurant's menu is, 'And can we order some crispy duck and prawn toast now?'

I love a bit of prawn toast, or Hatosie as it's known locally. I expect that prawn toast is a rather naff fast-food treat to those in the know, but it's one of my guilty pleasures. Actually, that whole guilty pleasure thing is a bit pathetic. People never actually reveal their deepest guilty pleasures. If I enjoyed smoking crack whilst wearing Speedos and listening to Supertramp, now that really would be a truly guilty pleasure, and not one I'd ever consider putting in a book. For the record, my top five printable guilty pleasures are:

1 . . . . Prawn toast (dipped in sweet chilli mayo = double naff)
2 . . . . The Carpenters' greatest hits
3 . . . . Spitting out chewing gum and trying to volley it over a fence
4 . . . . A string vest on a cold day
5 . . . . Cheddar cheese and strawberry jam sandwiches on sliced white 99

Prawn sesame toast

SERVES 4

FOR THE PRAWN TOAST

15 raw peeled king prawns (keep the shells for the Prawn and Coconut Bisque on page 35)

2 spring onions, thinly sliced

1 red bird's eye chilli, finely chopped

about 10 fresh coriander leaves

2 free-range egg whites

2 teaspoons soy sauce

pinch of salt

2 teaspoons cornflour

4 slices white bread

2 teaspoons sesame seeds (a mix of black and white is nice)

500ml vegetable oil

A Stupidly Simple Dip (see page 193), to serve

Put the peeled prawns into a food-processor along with the spring onion, chilli, coriander, egg white, soy sauce, salt and cornflour. Whizz it all up to a coarse paste and spread thickly and evenly onto the bread slices. Sprinkle with the sesame seeds and either chill in the fridge for up to 3 hours or cook immediately.

When you are ready to cook, heat the vegetable oil to 170°C in a pan that allows the oil to be at least 7cm deep. Lay the bread into the oil prawn-side down (you may need to fry the bread one slice at a time, depending on the size of your pan). The bread should start to fizz straight away. Cook for 2 minutes, then turn it over and give it another minute or so. Carefully lift the toasts out of the pan and drain on kitchen paper.

Cut the toasts into either fingers or mini triangles – this is completely up to you. I leave the crusts on, but if your friends are posher than mine (very likely), you don't have to. Serve with the Stupidly Simple Dip.

Author's note: If any young children are browsing this book, I have never smoked crack and would not encourage anyone to do so. If any middle-aged men are browsing this book – Speedos? Just don't! If anyone of my age is browsing this book, ain't nothing wrong with Supertramp!

> In Zanzibar, enterprising street-food sellers convert their bicycles into barbecues with pedals. They cycle these machines into Stone Town and fire up the coals. Most of the delicacies come on a skewer, and my favourite is this spicy chicken version. Now, I'm not sure if I have the exact recipe – in fact I suspect the original recipe may change according to what's available – but back in Blighty I set about recreating what I'd eaten and I reckon it's almost as good. And, no, I haven't converted my bicycle...yet.
>
> These skewers are ideal for a barbecue, or you can cook them indoors in a griddle pan or a non-stick frying pan. I am merely suggesting that you serve these with Mango & Red Pepper Jam and a few Plantain Crisps, but if you like these suggestions see pages 192 and 187 respectively. The first thing to do is visit your butcher and ask him to mince the chicken breast for you. You could chop the chicken by hand – and in Zanzibar I bet they do – but frankly, life's too short.

Spiced chicken skewers with plantain crisps, mango & red pepper jam

MAKES 20 SKEWERS (4 WOULD SATISFY A VERY HUNGRY, MILDLY GREEDY PERSON!)

30 cashew nuts

1kg chicken breast, minced

2 free-range eggs

4 teaspoons ground cumin

½ teaspoon salt

3 teaspoons chilli powder

2 tablespoons vegetable oil

1 tablespoon fresh white breadcrumbs

4 teaspoons very finely grated ginger

80g fresh coriander leaves, finely chopped

3 teaspoons garam masala

1 onion, very finely chopped

1 teaspoon white pepper

Soak 20 wooden skewers in warm water to prevent them from burning (particularly important if you intend to chargrill or barbecue the skewers). Next assemble all the ingredients. I grind the cashew nuts in a pestle and mortar until they resemble breadcrumbs.

Bung the minced chicken breast into a bowl. Whisk the eggs with the cumin, salt, chilli powder and oil and add to the chicken. Mix to combine, then chuck in the breadcrumbs, cashew nuts, ginger, coriander, garam masala, onion and white pepper. Mix it all up and divide into 20 lumps.

Roll each lump into a sausage shape and thread a skewer through the centre so that you have a 'sausage' of spicy chicken at one end of the skewer. These can be left in the fridge until required.

When you're ready, simply take a few skewers and cook, in batches if necessary, on a barbecue or fry in a griddle pan or non-stick frying pan over a high heat for about 8 minutes, or until cooked through, turning occasionally. If you're cooking them in batches, keep the cooked ones warm in the oven but don't leave them unguarded because they smell fantastic and someone will steal one!

66 This could very easily have ended up in the Simple Supper Spice chapter, but it makes a good starter or snack too, so it's staying put. If by chance you ever invite me over for Sunday dinner, you may wish to know that my favourite roast is slow-roasted pork belly (must have plenty of Bramley apple sauce), and if in the unlikely event I leave before it's all finished, this is what you must make the next day. Of course you might prefer roast beef, but that shouldn't prevent you from enjoying this salad, so I've given an easy roasting method with a bespoke piece of belly.

Pork belly is wonderful because it's so fatty and the fat packs all the flavour. Because it's fatty, it's generally paired up with something tart, such as the aforementioned Bramley apple sauce, or in this case pineapple. The pineapple could be thrown in completely raw and you would still have a very reasonable salad, but oven-drying or dehydrating changes the texture and intensifies the flavour. You are also taking tentative steps into the world of high-end molecular gastronomy, which will give us something to discuss if I do come round for that Sunday lunch, because I know nothing about high-end molecular gastronomy and I'm keen to learn! Finally, a quick heads-up on the dressing. It's a very important part of the salad and is definitely best warmed through before serving to really release all of the flavours. 99

Salad of pork belly, oven-dried pineapple & shiitake mushrooms

SERVES 4

600g boneless pork belly

2 teaspoons salt

4 decent slices from a sweet, ripe pineapple

olive oil, for frying

about 12 shiitake mushrooms, thickly sliced

2 little gem lettuces, each cut into 6–8 wedges

10 long sprigs of fresh coriander

12 stems tenderstem broccoli, cooked and cooled

If your pork is raw, you will need to cook and cool it before the salad fest. If using precooked leftovers, skip the cooking bit and simply cut the pork into bite-sized chunks.

Preheat the oven to 160°C/gas mark 3. Place the pork skin-side up on a baking tray and rub the salt into the skin. Cook for an hour, or until the meat is tender and has a lovely roasty colour. Don't panic if the skin hasn't crisped up – it isn't necessary at this stage. Leave the pork to cool, then cut into bite-sized chunks.

The pineapple also needs a little while in the oven but unfortunately at a different temperature from the pork, so you'll need to cook them separately. Sorry about that. Remove the skin from the pineapple slices and cut each one into about 12 wedges. Place a wire rack on a baking tray and spread the pineapple out on the rack. The very best way of cooking the pineapple would be to leave it in the oven overnight on the very lowest possible temperature – at the restaurant we do this on the oven pilot light. Second best is setting your oven at 50–100°C/gas mark ¼ and giving the pineapple about 2 hours. Keep an eye on it, because we don't want it to colour. It should wither and

FOR THE DRESSING

1 teaspoon black bean paste

2 teaspoons cracked black pepper

pinch of chilli flakes

1 tablespoon soy sauce

2½ tablespoons sweet chilli sauce

1½ teaspoons white wine vinegar

juice of 1 lime

20g caster sugar

15g fresh ginger, peeled and grated

2 tablespoons water

2 garlic cloves, finely chopped

50ml olive oil

dry but remain yellow. It will be chewy and a little shrivelled and basically dried when ready. It can be stored for a day or two in the fridge if not immediately used.

With these bits done you are ready to go.

Heat a frying pan and add a touch of oil. Add the pork belly chunks and fry them for about 5 minutes or until brown and crisp. Tip them into a bowl. Fry the mushrooms until caramelised and add these to the pork. Chuck in the lettuce wedges, coriander, broccoli and pineapple.

Heat all the dressing ingredients together in a small pan until just warmed (but not hot), spoon over the salad and serve.

MACE & NUTMEG

These both come from the same plant – the nutmeg tree. Hanging from the tree is the nutmeg fruit, which are far less commonly available than mace or nutmeg themselves. At the heart of the fruit is the nutmeg, and woven around the nutmeg is the mace. Both are usually bought dried and separate from one another, and both are widely used in both sweet and savoury dishes. Incidentally, you may have read that nutmeg is capable of producing a 'high' – back in my college days myself and two friends smoked my mum's entire supply of ground nutmeg, and absolutely nothing happened at all. Well, that's not strictly true – I was grounded for a month, but we didn't get high. It does turn out that the information had some basis of truth, but frankly it's not a reason for buying it!

I certainly don't want to give the impression that this section is all about dinner-party food. Personally, I have every reason to discourage dinner parties because I think you should go to a (my) restaurant on special occasions, always eating the full three courses (plus cheese), and choosing only the finest (expensive) wines. No, this section is about dishes that could be part of a bigger, more extravagant meal, but are equally fine being served up and eaten as they come. Contrary to many modern cookery writers, I believe that most cooks actually enjoy cooking, and so the following pages contain some dishes which require a bit of hard graft, but don't let that put you off. I'm with you all the way and have tried to indicate how you can chop some of the recipes down into stages and prepare bits in advance, thus making the cooking times seem a little less like hard work! Many of these dishes require nothing else to serve alongside; however, a few may ask you to detour to other parts of the book where a suitable suggested addition is given in more detail.

Spicing up your lunch & dinner

> Laksa is usually classified as a soup, but it's not a lightweight affair suitable only as a starter. A laksa is a meal in itself – that's certainly how I serve it. Chinese-Malay in origin, laksa comes in various styles, forms and flavours. This version is known as a curry laksa. The defining features of a laksa are the rice noodles, the tofu, the laksa paste and the coconut sauce. Now I confess I used to be a bit anti-tofu. I always gave it a wide berth, considering it some sort of odd, bland, diet-conscious vegetarian substance. In a way, it is all of those things, but it's also much more than that. Fried into puffs, it takes on a great texture and being rather subtle- (not bland)-tasting it absorbs other flavours extremely well. Fried tofu puffs (or curd puffs) can be bought ready done, but if you can't find them, buy a block of tofu, cut it into cubes and deep-fry it until golden brown.

Butternut & tofu laksa

SERVES 4

300g bean sprouts

2 heads bok choi, coarsely shredded

50g unsalted peanuts

2 tablespoons vegetable oil

½ butternut squash, diced into
    3cm cubes

600ml coconut milk

300ml water

20 curry leaves

1 tablespoon sugar

good pinch of salt

160g dried white rice noodles

250g fried tofu puffs

about 20 basil leaves, ripped and torn

about 15 mint leaves, ripped and torn

about 30 coriander leaves,
    ripped and torn

3 limes

FOR THE LAKSA PASTE

3 large red chillies

2 banana shallots, chopped

30g fresh ginger, peeled and chopped

2 garlic cloves, chopped

1 teaspoon basic curry powder

1–2 tablespoons water

First make the laksa paste. Place all of the paste ingredients into a food-processor and blend to a smooth paste. Set aside in the fridge.

Both the bean sprouts and the bok choi would be best precooked. Bring a small pan of water to the boil and chuck in the bean sprouts. Stir them around for 30 seconds and then fish them out with a slotted spoon and dunk them into a bowl of cold water to halt the cooking process. Then do exactly the same with the shredded bok choi. Drain the bean sprouts and bok choi and keep in the fridge for now.

Heat a frying pan over a medium heat and chuck in the peanuts. Let them colour slightly all over, leave to cool and then coarsely crush them in a pestle and mortar. Set aside. Add 1 tablespoon oil to the frying pan and fry the butternut until just softened and golden-coloured all over – 7–8 minutes.

Place a wok over the biggest heat source on your stovetop and add the remaining vegetable oil. Tip in the laksa paste and fry gently for 5 minutes, stirring occasionally. Pour in the coconut milk and the water and bring to a simmer. Bash up the curry leaves in your pestle and mortar and chuck these into the wok. Add the sugar and salt.

Put the noodles into a bowl and pour over enough boiling water to cover them. Allow them to steep for 3–4 minutes before draining off. The noodles will be translucent and soft.

Now find your serving bowls – I suggest wide shallow bowls, allowing you to see all of the different elements in the soup. Divide the noodles amongst the four bowls. Scatter the tofu into the bowls. Now back to the actual soup in the wok. The next bit must all happen very quickly – within a minute: chuck in the butternut, the bean shoots, bok choi and half the amount of each herb. Halve the limes and squeeze in all the juice. Place a squeezed lime half in each person's bowl. Pour the hot soup over the noodles and tofu in the bowls. Scatter over the peanuts and the remaining herbs and serve.

Several years ago I was aboard a small 12-person plane bound for Zanzibar. This was my first trip back to the island as an adult. As we approached the tiny dot in the Indian Ocean, I could feel a strong sense of 'belonging' to this exotic island. I was born in 1967 in Dar-es-Salaam, the capital of Tanzania. I would have been born in Zanzibar, but there had been a revolution on the island a couple of years before and as a result the hospitals were still in a state of disarray. Back in Zanzibar we lived in a big white house with three floors and a fabulous veranda overlooking the crystal-clear waters that surround the island, and Stone Town, the centre of the island's capital, was only a short walk away.

My dad was a marine biologist stationed at the East African Marine Fisheries Organisation. My mum had stopped work to care for what she rightly believed to be the most charming, beautiful baby ever born. We only lived on Zanzibar for a short while after my birth, but the island remained a very special place to our family and I felt a strong urge to return and explore the place as an adult. My cooking has been very much affected by our time abroad. Spice is the prevailing theme in Zanzibar, but how each spice is used depends on one's personal heritage – Persian, Arabic, Chinese, African and Indian foods are all common and reflect a very colourful history. Each time I have cooked a spicy dish on telly or in a magazine I have always mentioned Zanzibar in glowing terms.

The island's population is tiny and the list of inhabitants that have gone on to achieve any level of fame is very small. In fact I come in second, just behind Freddie Mercury, which shows you just how short the list is! So it did cross my mind that news of my constant 'upselling' of this fabulous place may have filtered back to the Zanzibari authorities, and that I would probably be driven from the airport to Stone Town in a cavalcade with gunmen firing volleys of celebration into the air. As it happened, they arranged a completely different surprise reception. They sent a local taxi driver who cunningly managed to take a 32-mile version of the 7-mile journey to Stone Town and stripped me of most of my holiday money before I'd even arrived.

Although the island's cuisine is multinational, the list of ingredients isn't huge. This is a small island in the middle of the Indian Ocean, after all. Fish plays a big part, and each day dhow boats leave the shore, returning hours later with an array of amazing species. Another ingredient that is hard to miss is coconut, and of course spices are everywhere. Zanzibar's biggest export is cloves. This dish is not a very precise Zanzibar recipe. It is my take on a dish we ate time and again and I've loosely based it on one my mum makes called 'kuku aku paku', or chicken in coconut milk. The choice of fish is up to you – I have made some suggestions, but the sauce is the important bit. I would suggest serving this with sticky rice and a salad.

Zanzibar-style fish curry

SERVES 4–6   RECIPE OVERLEAF ⟶

Zanzibar-style fish curry

CONTINUED FROM PAGE 65

1 whole fish, about 500g,
   (mullet, bass, bream
   or tilapia would all
   work well), scaled and gutted

500g mussels in the shell

12 raw king prawns in the shell

2½ teaspoons cumin seeds

2 teaspoons coriander seeds

6 cardamom pods, outer husks
   removed

2 cloves

½ teaspoon ground turmeric

vegetable oil, for frying

2 large onions, very finely chopped

5 garlic cloves, very finely chopped

5cm piece of fresh ginger,
   peeled and grated

3 green bird's eye chillies,
   2 thinly sliced into rings
   and 1 left whole

4 medium tomatoes, very finely diced

800ml coconut milk

150ml chicken or fish stock

juice of ½ lime

small bunch of basil

pinch of salt (optional)

Chill the fish, mussels and prawns in the fridge while you prepare the sauce. Grind the cumin seeds, coriander seeds, cardamom and cloves to a fine powder in a pestle and mortar. Add the ground turmeric and set aside.

Heat a glug of vegetable oil in a large casserole pot over a medium heat. Tip in the onions, garlic, ginger and the sliced chillies (leave the whole one for now). Cook for 1 minute, stirring. Add the tomatoes and sizzle for 1 minute. Add the spice mix and pour in the coconut milk and the stock.

Bring to a simmer and cook for about 20 minutes or until slightly thickened. At this stage you could cool and refrigerate the sauce for a couple of days, then reheat it when you are ready to cook the fish, or just proceed straight to the finish line.

Take the whole gutted fish out of the fridge and chop off its head. Cut the body into 4 large, even chunks, cutting straight through the bone. Add the fish chunks, mussels and prawns to the simmering sauce and cook for around 6 minutes or until the fish lifts away from the bone easily, the mussels have opened and the prawns are pink.

Grind the whole chilli in a pestle and mortar and add to the pan. Squeeze in the lime juice, tear up the basil and stir into the curry. Have a taste and add the salt if necessary. Serve immediately.

A NOTE ON THE FISH

OPTIONS

This dish would work very well with sea bass, sea bream, large mullet or snapper. As a guide, a 450g whole fish would generously feed two people. Ask your fishmonger to prepare the fish for you – he needs to scale it, trim off the fins and remove the guts. As with all fish, insist that it's as fresh as possible. Buy it on the day you intend to eat it if you can.

66 This is a fantastic dish both to cook and to eat, but before we go any further we need to clear up one small issue – whole fish have bones. I say this because we occasionally cook a whole fish at the restaurant and every time we do, you can guarantee that someone will summon the waiter and inform him that there is a problem with the whole fish we have just served.

'Excuse me, waiter, this whole baked bass has bones in it.'

'Er, right, yes, I'll take it back to the kitchen.'

'Chef, table 4 says there are bones in this fish.'

'You don't say. It's a whole fish – of course it's got bones in it!'

'But what shall I tell him?'

'Tell him if he can catch one without bones, I'll cook it for free.'

Okay, rant over.

A whole baked fish plonked on the table with a funky broth on the side looks pretty darn impressive, but is actually very simple and straightforward. You have options on the type of fish you can use (see left), and if it's a fish you've caught yourself (or if you can get away with fibbing), the dish becomes more impressive still. The broth served with the fish was inspired by a dish I had cooked for me (I say me; there were about 70 people in the restaurant, but you know what I mean) by a very highly regarded American chef famous for his Mexican-inspired cuisine. Making the broth is interesting because you will taste the layers of flavour stacking up as each ingredient is added.

The fish can be marinated ahead of time and kept in the fridge until required. It will take around about 30 minutes to cook in the oven and should be served straight away (rather than have it sit around whilst your guests make light work of your finest gin and the green olives you found in the cupboard). The broth is best made and served immediately, so I would suggest getting all the broth ingredients ready well ahead of time, meaning you can prepare it whilst the fish bakes. 99

Whole baked sea bass with wok-fried peppers & a citrus, chilli & coriander broth

SERVES 4

1 large or 2 small sea bass, about 1kg, scaled and gutted

olive oil, for roasting and drizzling

2 tablespoons oyster sauce

2 tablespoons soy sauce

4 teaspoons demerara sugar

2 sprigs of thyme, leaves only, finely chopped

Begin by marinating the sea bass. Lay the fish on a chopping board and, using your sharpest knife, slash the fish five times on either side across the body to make incisions around 3mm deep. Have a large non-stick roasting tin at the ready, big enough for the fish but small enough to fit in your oven (I know it's obvious, but there will be someone ...). Slosh a glug of the olive oil into the tray and spread evenly. Mix the oyster sauce, soy sauce, sugar and thyme leaves together in a small bowl and spoon the mixture into the incisions, then plonk the fish into the tin. Drizzle a touch more olive oil over the fish and chill in the fridge until your guests have arrived. When you are ready to cook, preheat the oven to 175°C/gas mark 4 and cook the fish for 30 minutes for 1 large fish, or around 10 minutes if you are using 2 smaller fish.

MORE INGREDIENTS OVERLEAF ...

CONTINUED OVERLEAF... ⟶

Whole baked sea bass with wok-fried peppers & a citrus, chilli & coriander broth

CONTINUED FROM PAGE 67

FOR THE CITRUS, CHILLI &
CORIANDER BROTH

olive oil, for stir-frying

2 red peppers, deseeded and
thinly sliced

2 yellow peppers, deseeded and
thinly sliced

1 red chilli, deseeded and sliced
into very fine rings

1 green chilli, deseeded and sliced
into very fine rings

80g fresh ginger, peeled and grated

6 garlic cloves, finely chopped

425ml fish or chicken stock (I prefer
to use chicken, but it's your call)

grated zest of 1 orange and juice to
taste

grated zest of 1 lime and juice to taste

grated zest of 1 lemon and juice to
taste

1½ teaspoons caster sugar

pinch of salt

1 small bunch of fresh coriander,
about 80g, finely shredded

That's really about it on the fish front apart from to say that in my professional world I would commission an eager chef to flip the fish over halfway through the cooking time, to make sure both sides benefited from the dry heat of the oven, whereas at home I'd think about it and then think nahhh, it'll be ok. Your call.

Now for the broth. Bear in mind that you are possibly going to be cooking this in front of your guests, so hide this book (though do recommend it enthusiastically to them after supper), look confident and everything will be fine. Heat a good glug of olive oil in a wok over a high heat until nice and hot. Chuck in the peppers and stir-fry for 1 minute until slightly softened but not coloured. Add the chillies, ginger and garlic and toss them around for a minute or two so they begin to cook. Pour in the stock and gently nudge all of the bits down so they are fully submerged. Reduce the heat to medium-low and bring the stock to a gentle simmer. Have a taste – you will get the garlicky, gingery peppers and quite a distinct fishy flavour (if you are using fish stock) along with a good tingle from the chillies.

Chuck in the citrus zest and stir, taste once again – you should now notice a real zing to the flavour – then add the sugar to give an important layer of sweetness (you can say all this out loud to your guests if you want – they'll be impressed!). Squeeze in the juice of half the orange, lemon and lime and taste. If you want increased citrus, add more juice (I suspect you'll want a bit more, but maybe not all of the lemon juice). Add the salt, stir through the coriander and serve up straight away.

I suggest serving the broth in a big pot with a ladle and transferring the whole fish to a large serving dish and letting everyone scrape off its flesh and pour over their own broth. Spinach or green beans would do as a vegetable side, and if anyone mentions fish bones…

“ I'm indulging myself here, I admit. Many chefs, myself included, look back at dishes from five or ten years previously and cringe a little. It's a bit like flicking through your teenage record collection. But this particular dish has appeared at every restaurant I've been in charge of – it's adapted itself to each venue but essentially remains the same. I like it as much now as I did back then. Bass is the ideal fish for this dish because it can be cooked hard and fast in a hot pan. It's worth mentioning that wild bass is infinitely better than farmed, if you can get hold of it or happen to know a decent fisherman. This is more a set of directions for assembly rather than an actual recipe, so apologies in advance for the references to recipes on other pages, which makes cooking it a little more complicated. You could always pop into the restaurant and let me cook it for you. ”

Pan-fried sea bass on sag aloo & onion bhajis with curry oil & tomato chilli jam

SERVES 4

1½ tablespoons vegetable oil

1 onion, finely chopped

1 tablespoon hot curry powder

300ml olive oil

4 sea bass fillets, each about 170g, cut in half

200ml natural yogurt

1 quantity Sag Aloo (see page 197)

1 quantity Onion Bhajis (see page 198)

1 quantity Tomato Chilli Jam (see page 190)

First make a curry oil. Heat a frying pan over a medium heat, add 1 tablespoon of the vegetable oil and fry the onion until golden brown, then mix in the curry powder. Pour in the olive oil and allow to simmer for 10 minutes. Remove from the heat and leave the infused oil to cool, stirring occasionally. Pass the oil through a fine sieve or a sheet of muslin, then store the oil in the fridge until needed.

Heat a non-stick frying pan over a high heat, add the remaining vegetable oil and cook the sea bass fillets, skin-side down, until the skin colours slightly and starts to crisp up. Turn the fish over and cook a little more gently on the other side.

Fleck four plates with a little natural yogurt – the yogurt will add a nice mellow contrast to the stronger flavours. Warm up the sag aloo and spoon some into a pastry cutter (this is a very cheffy manoeuvre but we are replicating a restaurant dish here – otherwise, just place a few spoonfuls on the plate). Pop a sea bass fillet on top of each portion of sag aloo.

Fry the onion bhajis and divide equally between the plates, placing them on top of the sea bass. Spoon a dollop of Tomato Chilli Jam on top of the bhajis and drizzle a little infused curry oil around the plate.

You could of course simply cook the bass and serve all the other bits on the side – it would taste just the same!

Thailand, April 2011... so, take a fillet of bass (you could use bream, mullet or even haddock, I guess) and cut it into 6 chunks. Toss the chunks in flour, throw them into hot oil and fry them up (a Frenchman would weep to see bass deep-fried in this way!). When the fish is cooked, the outside should be crispy and the inside moist, hot and sweet. Place the fish into a bowl with some wedges of really ripe tomato and a few coriander leaves, and now the sucker punch – pour over a cold dressing made of fresh lime juice, fish sauce, crushed fresh mint, raw shallots, thinly sliced lemongrass and chilli paste.

I'm not sure if this is exactly what we ate last night, but through a sort-of conversation with a Thai restaurant owner involving quite a lot of mime, and good old detective work, I reckon it's pretty close. It's also an excellent example of how I write most of my recipes. This recipe is being typed at 7am on a beautiful Thai island called Khol Khud, 150 miles from the mainland. Last night I went with my family around the coast in a speed-boat and up a narrow inlet to a wooden shack on stilts where we sat at a low table on big cushions, watching the sun go down on one side whilst a large jolly Thai lady cooked with chilli and a smile on the other. I knew straight away that we were in for an incredible meal – one that would instantly rank in my top five dinners ever (I love a list). As yet I haven't made this dish, but from what I ate last night I know it's something I'm going to cook and eat again and again.

Fried fish with rice noodles, chilli, lemongrass & fresh herbs

SERVES 4

600ml vegetable oil

4 bream fillets, each cut into
　5–6 pieces across the fillet

handful of plain flour

300g straight-to-wok or precooked
　rice noodles

4 medium tomatoes, cut into 8 wedges

4 spring onions, thinly sliced on
　an angle

⅓ medium cucumber, halved
　lengthways, deseeded and
　thinly sliced

1 banana shallot, thinly sliced
　into rings

2 little gem lettuces, cut into 8 wedges

3 tablespoons roughly chopped fresh
　coriander

2 tablespoons roughly chopped basil

10 mint leaves, roughly chopped

Crispy Shallots (see page 186),
　to serve

FOR THE DRESSING

½ lemongrass stalk, very thinly
　sliced into rings

10g fresh ginger, peeled and grated

3 garlic cloves, roughly chopped

1–2 red bird's eye chillies, roughly
　chopped, seeds and all!

1½ tablespoons fish sauce

juice of 2 limes

1 tablespoon caster sugar

First, make the dressing, which can be done well before tea time and even a day or two in advance. Grind and pound the lemongrass, ginger, garlic and chillies (with plenty of aggression) in a pestle and mortar until they form a coarse paste. Add the fish sauce, lime juice and sugar and stir well. Have a taste – it should be powerfully spicy. Look for the individual flavours and redress the balance between hot, sweet, sour and salty, if you feel the need, by adding a little extra of any of the ingredients. Dressing done.

The next bit is done 'to order', as we professional types say. The best approach is to have all the ingredients prepared and ready to go.

Heat the oil in a pan. Use one that is deep enough to hold about 5cm of oil with at least 7cm of pan left above it, to allow for the frying, bubbling fish. Heat the oil until it's about 175°C (see the note on useful equipment on page 14). Toss the pieces of fish in the flour and shake off any excess. I recommend cooking the fish in two batches so the temperature of the oil stays nice and hot. Lower the first batch of fish into the pan using a slotted spoon – it should bubble and hiss in the hot oil straight away. Allow to cook for 3–4 minutes until it is a little crusty and pale golden on the outside, then lay it on some kitchen paper. Repeat with the remaining fish.

The plan now is to mix the hot fish with the remaining ingredients and serve as quickly as possible, so don't answer the telephone or pour another glass of wine. Focus!

Place the noodles in a large, wide serving dish or bowl. Add the tomatoes, spring onions, cucumber, shallot, lettuce, coriander, basil and mint. Place the fish on top. Pour over half the dressing and very gently turn everything over a couple of times to mix. Don't overwork it and be careful not to break up the fish.

Serve in bowls with the remaining dressing and Crispy Shallots on the side for people to add as they wish.

Steamed fish might sound a little drab but is actually a fabulous way of enjoying the real flavour of fish. Not all fish is perfect for steaming – oily chaps such as mackerel, herring or trout need that caramelisation from a hot frying pan, I think, but halibut, sea bass, brill, turbot and salmon can all be steamed very successfully. A quick word on halibut: if you can afford to use wild halibut, that is definitely the way to go, but a farmed version is available and usually considerably cheaper. Wild halibut can grow very large, so don't ask for 'one whole halibut, please,' or you could end up eating the same fish for a very long time… and have to sell the family silver to pay for it! Request your fish by weight – 160g of boneless halibut fillet per person is a generous portion. The best kit for steaming fish is the oriental-style bamboo basket that sits on top of a pan of boiling water. Some cooks like to flavour up the water with black beans, spices, herbs, or wines and vinegars – personally I don't think it makes any difference, but you're welcome to try. This dish feels vaguely Japanese to me – I'm certainly not saying it's authentic in any way, but there's a purity and simplicity of flavour that is of a Japanese style.

Steamed halibut with prawn toast & green pea & wasabi purée

SERVES 4

2 slices of Prawn Sesame Toast – (see page 55)

275g frozen peas

up to 25g wasabi paste

150ml water

4 portions of halibut, each about 160g

about a teaspoon of sea salt flakes

baby cress (optional poncy cheffy customisation)

1 tablespoon kejap manis (see opposite)

First of all, have a look at the prawn toast recipe on page 55, just so you know what to buy and what the recipe entails. You could make your prawn toast mix several hours in advance. The pea and wasabi purée can also be made and chilled and then reheated as required, so I shall start with that part of the recipe.

Bring a pan of water to the boil and chuck in the peas. Let them simmer for 2 minutes and then pour them into a strainer and from there into your blender. Immediately start the blender working (we want to maintain the fantastic green colour, so working quickly through the stages is important). Once the peas have blended for about 2 minutes, stop the machine and add the wasabi paste and the water before blending for a further 2 minutes – this should leave you with a very smooth, very green purée with a fairly loose consistency. Have a taste: look for the sweetness of the peas but also the fiery kick of wasabi. If in doubt, add more wasabi – it's an important flavour in the overall dish. Add a little more water if you think the purée is too claggy.

(If you choose to cool your pea purée for later use, pour it into a large container and shove it in the fridge to cool it down as quickly as possible. A microwave is the best way of reheating the purée.) So your purée is made and your prawn toast mix is ready to spread on bread and fry, which means you are free to cook the fish when required.

Take a bamboo steamer basket and place your halibut portions inside, sprinkle over the flaked salt and put the lid on the basket. Place the basket over a pan of simmering water. A snug fit will ensure that all the steam filters through into the basket. It's very difficult to say exactly how long your fish will steam for, but expect it to take 5–10 minutes.

Once it is ready, you should serve the halibut as soon as possible, so make sure that your prawn toast is cooked, your pea purée is hot and that you have the kejap manis close by. You are free to serve up however you wish, but if a cheffy, plated version appeals, here's what I do: swipe the pea purée across each plate by putting a generous dessertspoon dollop on one side of the plate and then dragging the spoon through the dollop, drawing the purée across.

Place your prawn toast across the purée and your bass on top of the prawn toast. Sprinkle over a few cress leaves, if using, and finally trickle a little kejap manis from the tip of a spoon across the plate.

Kejap manis is a sweet, sticky soy sauce from Indonesia – it's sweetened and thickened with palm sugar. In the restaurant we sometimes flick and swirl it, in a dramatic, artistic fashion (or so we think!), over a finished dish. If you intend to use it, bear in mind how sweet it is.

KEJAP MANIS

> In Britain, it's a long-accepted fact that a restaurateur can charge extra for any dish with a French word in the title. Chicken pithivier with *pomme purée* is worth so much more to the average punter than a simple chicken pie and mash. Likewise, if one were to serve an apple tart with custard, it would not have the same effect on gross profit as serving the very same apple tart with *crème anglaise*. I'm not sure this theory extends to other lanuages, but you'll note I slipped a little Spanish into the title in the hope that I may be able to nudge the price of the book northwards a touch. It's worth a try in these tough economic times. This dish is a corker and well worth the price of the book alone. It's very easy to make and guaranteed to please. *Patatas bravas* are, very simply, fried potatoes. But hang on! Since the world of cooking went all test tubes and lab coats, it turns out that frying potatoes is anything but simple. We shall ponder this more during the recipe.
>
> *Pimenton ahumado* is smoked paprika – a spice that turns up again and again in Spanish cookery. The finest producers of smoked paprika smoke their peppers over oak fires before grinding them down into a fine powder. Aioli is similar to mayonnaise but not interchangeable. It's an obscenely garlicky emulsified sauce served with all sorts of things. Don't skip this element!
>
> And finally the prawns...I cook them in the shell because I think it preserves flavour that would otherwise be discarded. Personally I don't bother peeling seared prawns and I eat the shell as well, but my daughter Ellie tells me that makes me strange. Not funny-strange or cool, mysterious strange. Just strange.

Seared prawns with patatas bravas, chilli, garlic & pimenton ahumado & aioli

SERVES 4

4 medium potatoes, cut into 2cm dice

6 tablespoons olive oil

16 large raw king prawns in the shell

100g unsalted butter

4 really ripe plum tomatoes, finely diced

4 garlic cloves, finely chopped

2 red chillies, finely diced

1 teaspoon sea salt

2 teaspoons smoked paprika

juice of ½ lemon

1 tablespoon chopped flat-leaf parsley

TO SERVE

1 huge fresh white baguette

1 quantity Aioli (see opposite)

Bring a large pan of water to the boil and tip in the potatoes. Bring to a simmer and cook gently, to prevent the potatoes from breaking up, until cooked through. Test one, and if you can easily crush it with a fork, they're ready. Drain the potatoes, but DON'T cool them in cold water. Allow them to steam away, in a dish, until they have cooled completely. The idea here is to rid the inside of the potato of any water, and that escaping steam is water... well, it's steam, but it was water, and would still be water trapped inside had you cooled them under running cold water!

The serious point about the cooling method is this: if you were to fry the potatoes with water still trapped inside, the water would heat up again during the frying and try to escape through the sides of the crisping potatoes, causing them to go soggy. Anyway, potato lecture over. To recap, at this point you should have steaming, cooling potatoes. When they're cold, chill them in the fridge until needed. Let's move on...

Apart from the potatoes, everything else is basically cooked to order (not counting the aioli, which needs to be made ahead of time). Heat 4 tablespoons of the oil in a frying pan. Add the cold potatoes and fry them until golden and crispy all over. Tip the potatoes out onto a tray covered with kitchen paper to drain.

Return the pan to a high heat and add the remaining oil. Lay the prawns in the pan and cook for 2 minutes on either side. If the prawns catch slightly, that's great and will add additional flavour! Add in the butter – it will melt and seethe, but try to prevent it from burning. Immediately add the tomatoes. The moisture from the tomatoes will sizzle and evaporate, which is good. Continue to cook for 3 minutes.

Chuck in the garlic, chillies, salt and paprika. Sizzle for 1 minute, then tip the crispy potatoes back into the pan. Squeeze over the lemon juice and finish with the parsley. Toss everything together to make sure those powerful flavours mingle. Serve in bowls with crusty bread and aioli on the side.

66 There are those who put chopped garlic into mayonnaise and call it aioli – no, no and no! Aioli is a very garlicky Spanish sauce bearing a resemblance to mayonnaise, but it should be made with olive oil and without the mayonnaise-like additions of mustard or vinegar.

Years ago I spent the summer in San Sebastian with a friend who worked at a fabulous, highly acclaimed restaurant. Being in our early twenties, we spent most evenings drinking beer and trying to chat up the beautiful local Basque girls, and by the end of each night we would be drunk but very single. We would then make our way to a late-night bar for more beer and amazingly simple but tasty, crusty baguettes filled with chargrilled chicken slathered in garlic aioli. Not the intended end to the evening, but very satisfying nonetheless. 99

Aioli

MAKES ENOUGH FOR 8 DECENT SERVINGS

5 garlic cloves

1 teaspoon salt

4 egg yolks

180ml olive oil (I use a reasonably cheap, light-tasting oil for this)

1 teaspoon smoked paprika

Bash the garlic and salt together in a pestle and mortar, then transfer to a bowl.

Add the egg yolks and whisk, then gradually whisk in the olive oil and finally the smoked paprika. Your finished aioli will be a similar consistency to shop-bought mayonnaise, but bear in mind it will 'set up' in the fridge.

" Just say I had a lovely gastro pub close to Richmond Park in London with roaring log fires, charming waiters, a fabulous menu, an award-winning wine list and competitive prices…and just say the phone number was 020 8876 4238… you could book a table and come in and try this particular dish because it has gastro pub-type food written all over it. Just say….

There are lots of different clams found the world over. Clams are defined as bi-valves, which to you and me means that they have two tightly closed shells. Have a chat with your fishmonger – they will know which edible clam types are available. Cook your clams on the day that you buy them and bear in mind that you are only getting 25 per cent of the purchased weight in edible meat – the rest is shell. I usually allow 250g of raw in-the-shell clams per person for a starter and 500g for a main course. This is the sort of dish that needs to be cooked and eaten straight away, so have your guests sitting *in situ* whilst you do the cooking. "

Clams cooked in cider with smoked bacon, chorizo, parsley & chilli

SERVES 4

1 tablespoon vegetable oil

12 rashers dry-cure smoked bacon, finely shredded

200g chorizo, broken into smallish chunks

2kg fresh live clams in the shell

850ml cider

2 red chillies, thinly sliced into rings

4 garlic cloves, finely chopped

2 shallots, thinly sliced into rings

2 tablespoons coarsely chopped flat-leaf parsley

pinch of salt

Once you have assembled all the ingredients, the cooking is fun, fast and furious. Select a nice large pan for which you have a lid. Heat the pan over a high heat until good and hot. Pour in the vegetable oil and let it get really hot. Tip in the bacon and chorizo and fry for 2 minutes.

Rinse the clams under cold water to remove any grit from the shells, drain and then tip them into the pot – they will immediately sizzle and steam dramatically. Give the pot a good shake around in a manly fashion. Slam the lid on aggressively. Your guests will be impressed.

Now lift the lid and pour in the cider. Slam the lid back on for 2 minutes, during which time the cider will start to boil, shaking the pan about a few times to mix up the clams. Lift the lid and chuck in the chillies, garlic and shallots and give everything a good stir up with a wooden spoon. Keep the liquid boiling during this process.

Finally stir in the parsley and salt and immediately pour the whole contents of the pan into a big serving dish and stick it in the middle of the table. Serve with a lot of crusty white bread on the side.

A WORD ON COOKING CLAMS

A lot of people worry about cooking shellfish, so just to clear things up… Always store your live shellfish in the fridge. Don't put them in water – they are salt-water creatures, so tap water is the last thing they want to sit in. Just before cooking the clams, give them a rinse in cold water to remove any grit on the shells and then sift through them. At this point discard any clam that is open – an open shell means that the animal inside is dead and not safe to eat. It's always worth tapping the shell to see if they slowly shut, because the cunning old clam might just be fooling around. Avoid eating any clams that have not opened during cooking as this again suggests that the clam may have popped its clogs ahead of time and is unfit for consumption. Broadly speaking, the same applies to mussels, by the way. Right, health and safety lecture over.

This is not so much a dish as a cooking method. Its origins are firmly Cajun and I came across it years ago whilst on a solo trip hunting alligators on the Mississippi. Or was it surfing the internet...definitely one of the two. Anyway, it's a fascinating cooking method. A layer of butter and a mix of pungent spices form a dark crust around the chicken breast as it cooks, which seals in all the juices, giving a wonderfully sweet and spicy meat. It's ideal for the barbecue or it can be cooked in a very hot, dry frying pan or skillet. Any rice dish would go very well with Blackened Chicken, or you can chop it up and toss through a salad with chargrilled vegetables, but my favourite way of having a Blackened Chicken fix is in a very fresh, crusty baguette and Mango & Red Pepper Jam (see page 192) and a bowl of homemade chips.

Blackened chicken

SERVES 4

1 teaspoon finely ground black pepper

½ teaspoon finely ground white pepper

1 teaspoon garlic powder

1 teaspoon onion powder

1 teaspoon ground cumin

1 teaspoon cayenne pepper

½ teaspoon paprika

1 tablespoon salt

4 skinless and boneless chicken breasts

250g butter, melted

Mix all of the spices and the salt together in a bowl and set aside.

Take the chicken breasts and remove the skin completely. Also remove the wing bone that may still be attached. Lay the chicken on a piece of non-stick baking paper and carefully paint a layer of melted butter all over the surface of the chicken. The chicken will be cold because it's been in the fridge, so the butter will start to set quickly. Before this happens take several good pinches of the spice mix and sprinkle over the buttered chicken, so that it is completely coated in spice. Allow the butter to set for a few seconds.

Turn the chicken breasts over and do exactly the same to the other side. Be careful when manoeuvring the chicken, because the set butter will become brittle. At this stage the chicken can be chilled for up to an hour.

To cook the chicken, heat a large, heavy-based frying pan over a high heat. Don't be tempted to add any oil. Carefully lay the chicken breasts in the pan – my pan is 30cm in diameter and I cook 2 breasts at a time in it, but if yours is smaller, you may need to cook them separately as overcrowding the pan will result in disappointing 'blackening'. The pan will immediately smoke aggressively, and that's fine. Don't move the chicken – this harsh heat is important. After about 5 minutes, turn the chicken over to cook the other side. I use tongs to hold the chicken on its side so that I can blacken the edges, too. In total, the chicken breasts should take about 12 minutes to cook, but check that they are cooked through before serving – they can be finished in a hot oven if absolutely necessary.

"One of the major differences between the recipes I wrote for this book and the recipes I write in my professional life for the team in the kitchen is the tone and feel of the writing. Recipes for home cooks need to be written in a friendly, chatty, informative, arm-around-the-shoulder type way, not the 'bullet point' approach I take with my chefs in the restaurant. Hollandaise, for instance:

• Warm butter • Whisk yolks • Add reduction • Add butter • If it curdles, you're fired • Serve

This approach would fail completely in the competitive world of cookbook publishing. My editor Sophie would certainly call me up and tell me to 'pad out' my recipes with warm words of encouragement for the reader.

My staff, on the other hand, would find it very odd if I gave them a recipe written in the home cookbook style. They wouldn't be able to deal with all the fluffy, cuddly stuff. I can hear them now: 'Seen this recipe Chef gave me? Full of long words, praise, encouragement and warnings about hot pan-handles. I like aggressive bullet points and the occasional bollocking. The bloke's lost it, I reckon.'

When I decided to include the following recipe in this book, I was pleased to find that I had it typed up on my computer already. I thought that it was just a quick cut-and-paste job and then on to the next recipe. But no. When I opened the document I was horrified to find that I had summarised the entire recipe in 41 words spread over 6 tiny bullet points. So I've fleshed it out, written in lots of handy hints, occasional praise and lots of encouragement!

This recipe is a favourite of mine at home and in the restaurant, and it's perfect for a dinner party – simple to make, packed with flavour and you can prepare it in advance. Of course you don't have to wait until you are entertaining friends – feel free to eat it on a Wednesday night in front of the telly."

Smoked paprika chicken casserole with chickpeas, peppers & chorizo

SERVES 4

A QUICK WORD ABOUT THE INGREDIENTS

Not all chorizo sausage is created equal. As with so much in life, you get what you pay for. I use an Alejandro chorizo, which I buy from a specialist Spanish supplier, but supermarkets stock a variety of chorizos. Look out for a rustic cooking chorizo made of pork, paprika, garlic, seasoning and nothing else. This recipe also calls for chickpeas. If you can be bothered to soak and cook dried chickpeas, your casserole will be even better. I do at work; I don't at home.

CONTINUED OVERLEAF... ⟶

Smoked paprika chicken casserole with chickpeas, peppers & chorizo

CONTINUED FROM PAGE 83

3 tablespoons olive oil

1 large red onion, thinly sliced

large sprig of thyme

2 garlic cloves, thinly sliced

1 teaspoon fennel seeds

good pinch of chilli flakes

generous pinch of saffron

1 teaspoon smoked paprika

500g chorizo, diced

2 red peppers, thinly sliced

2 yellow peppers thinly sliced

3 plum tomatoes, cut into 8 wedges

1 tablespoon vegetable oil

2 chicken breasts, halved

4 chicken thighs

400g can chickpeas, rinsed and drained (or equivalent soaked and cooked dried chickpeas)

caster sugar, to taste (optional, depending on how ripe your tomatoes are)

salt and freshly ground black pepper

Heat half of the olive oil in a heavy-based, lidded casserole pot. Chuck in the onion, thyme and garlic and let everything sizzle in the hot oil for about 3 minutes or until softened but not coloured. Add the fennel seeds, chilli flakes, saffron and smoked paprika and stir.

Add the remaining olive oil and, when it has heated up a little, add the chorizo, peppers and tomato wedges. Sizzle for 5 minutes. Pour in half a mug of cold water, pop the lid on, reduce the heat to low and leave everything to stew gently for about 15 minutes.

Meanwhile, heat a large frying pan over a high heat, add the vegetable oil and cook the chicken, in batches if necessary, until sealed (when a chef asks you to seal something, all they want you to do is brown the outside rather than cooking it through). Set aside.

Back to the casserole. When you lift the lid you should find that the vegetables have all softened and the chorizo is cooked. If not, cook for a few minutes more. Tip in the chickpeas and stir, then add the chicken, pushing it into the stew. Put the lid back on and again leave to stew away for another 15 minutes or until the chicken is cooked through.

You are basically done, but have a taste. You may think it should be slightly sweeter, in which case add a pinch or two of sugar. I expect it will need a pinch of salt and a twist of pepper, too.

The options for serving this are varied. You could do some mash or new potatoes, but as the chickpeas are quite filling you may not need anything too heavy. I think the best additions are a slice of ciabatta fried in olive oil and a dollop of Aioli (see page 77).

One of my favourite local Indian restaurants has this dish on the menu. The last time I was there I asked for the recipe. The waiter went off to the kitchen, returning with more of a shopping list than a recipe, so I've played around a bit and I think I've got close!

This dish originates from Goa, a state in the south west of India. The local cuisine is now world famous due in no small part to the fact that Goa has a thriving tourist industry. Two particular flavours come up time and again: the sour, piquant flavour achieved through the use of vinegar, wine or tamarind, and the fiery heat of chillies and spice – both of which are present here. As with many curries, this dish really does benefit from being cooked a day in advance if you can bear holding out.

Murgh moelho

SERVES 4

2 tablespoons vegetable oil

12 chicken thighs

4 teaspoons cumin seeds

3 teaspoons yellow mustard seeds

good pinch of chilli flakes

1 teaspoon ground turmeric

2 teaspoons chilli powder

5 tablespoons white wine vinegar

2 onions, halved and thinly sliced

7 garlic cloves, crushed

250ml water

1 teaspoon salt

Heat a large frying pan over a high heat, add 1 tablespoon vegetable oil and fry the chicken thighs until they have a good roasty colour all over (you're not trying to cook them at this stage, so just cook until browned). The next job is a strange one. You need to select a knife with a nice sharp tip and prick the chicken thighs all over, making at least 15 small incisions in each thigh. Don't skip this bit as it helps the penetration of flavour as the chicken cooks. Set the chicken thighs aside.

Meanwhile, heat a small frying pan and dry-fry the cumin seeds, mustard seeds and chilli flakes until they release a strong aroma and start to brown very slightly. They may also pop as they heat up. Leave to cool, grind to a fine powder in a pestle and mortar, then mix in the turmeric and chilli powder. Pour the vinegar into a large bowl and stir in the spice mix.

Place the chicken thighs in the bowl with the vinegar and spice mix and give them a good old stir around, making sure the vinegar and spice are rubbed all over the chicken pieces. Leave this to one side for 20 minutes.

Heat a pan with a tightly-fitting lid over a medium-high heat and add the remaining slosh of vegetable oil. Tip in the onions and garlic and cook for 15 minutes or until they are a really dark brown. Add the chicken thighs, scraping in any spicy vinegar residue from the bowl. Pour in the water, add the salt and bring to a simmer. Reduce the heat to low, cover and cook for 45 minutes or until the chicken is tender and cooked through, the kitchen smells amazing and you are very hungry indeed. Resist! Tip the curry into an ovenproof dish and leave to cool, then cover and refrigerate overnight.

When you are ready to eat, simply preheat the oven to 160°C/gas mark 3 and put the dish in the oven for 25–30 minutes to reheat the curry. Serve with white Basmati rice.

> When I was kid I can recall my dad singing songs in the car as we drove around the countryside. This in itself is bad enough (I know, because my own children have complained when I've struck up a tune), but what made it much worse was that he only knew three songs which could even vaguely be described as contemporary popular music. One of these had been a big hit a few years before (quite a few years before!) for Fats Domino and was entitled 'Jambalaya (On the Bayou)'. The original version of this song is by Hank Williams and very much celebrates all things Cajun, particularly the cuisine. 'Jambalaya and a crawfish pie and filé gumbo' is how the chorus starts and, frankly, we could accuse old Hank of simply putting a tune to any number of local Cajun-Creole restaurant menus, but the bottom line is, he's provided me with a very nifty recipe intro and I'm grateful for that.
>
> Jambalaya is a rice dish made with peppers, onions, celery, chicken, sausage and seafood and, once cooked, it is often baked in the oven. I've only had Jambalaya once but really enjoyed it. Crawfish pie is exactly what it says on the tin (crawfish is like a lobster), leaving only filé gumbo requiring an explanation. Gumbo is a stew, which has a base of onions, celery and peppers (known locally as the Holy Trinity) and can contain meat or fish. Okra, hot sausage and spice are the other familiar characteristics.
>
> The word filé that Mr Williams uses in his song refers to the dried and ground leaves of the sassafras tree found in North America. This spice is also a useful thickening agent.
>
> Whilst gumbo has a very eclectic family tree – West African, Spanish and French – it is the official dish of the state of Louisiana and the main man in those parts is chef Paul Prudhomme. I was given his book many years ago and in it are various gumbo recipes, from catfish to squirrel and everything in between. The following recipe is my version of gumbo based on attempts at several of his! The dish is a labour of love, so make it when you are assured of an audience who will appreciate and applaud your efforts.
>
> Oh, and by the way, the other two songs my dad used to sing were 'Yellow Submarine' by The Beatles and 'Chirpy Chirpy Cheep Cheep' by Middle of the Road... I had a tough childhood!

Chicken gumbo
(son of a gun, we'll have big fun on the bayou)

SERVES 8 GENEROUSLY

FOR STAGE 1

2 large chickens, about 1.8kg each

6 garlic cloves, crushed to a purée with a little rock salt

1 tablespoon cayenne pepper

1 tablespoon ground black pepper

This recipe works best if broken down into stages.

Stage 1 is preparing and marinating the chicken. The day before you want to serve the dish, cut each whole chicken into six by dividing the drumsticks, thighs and breasts. Remove the skin from all the pieces and cut the breasts in half. To make the marinade, mix the garlic with the cayenne pepper and black pepper to form a paste. Set a quarter of the paste aside and rub the remainder all over the chicken pieces, rubbing really well, then chill for up to 24 hours.

MORE INGREDIENTS OVERLEAF ...

CONTINUED... ⟶

Chicken gumbo (son of a gun, we'll have big fun on the bayou)

CONTINUED FROM PAGE 87

FOR STAGE 2

600ml chicken stock

50g plain flour

50g butter

400g can chopped tomatoes

FOR STAGE 3

vegetable oil, for frying

1 onion, diced

1 green pepper, diced

4 celery sticks, sliced

2 good pinches of salt

3 teaspoons filé powder (found on the internet or specialist spice shops)

6 kabanos sausages, about 150g, cut into thickish slices (chorizo or similar cured sausage would work, too)

45g ham, diced

2 hard-boiled eggs, chopped

8 spring onions, sliced

200g okra, cut into 5mm slices

2 tablespoons chopped parsley

Stage 2 is the actual cooking bit and for this we need to make a simple version of a velouté sauce (to you and me that means a chicken sauce thickened with butter and flour). Pour the chicken stock into a large pan or casserole pot, cover and bring to a simmer. Rub the butter and flour together to form a paste. Drop small pellets of the flour and butter paste into the simmering chicken stock and whisk so that it breaks up and disperses. After a few minutes you should have a fairly smooth sauce with the consistency of double cream. Add the tomatoes and simmer for a further 10 minutes.

Meanwhile, heat a non-stick frying pan and add the marinated chicken pieces. Fry until they take on a golden-brown colour (they will still be raw inside at this point). Drop the sealed chicken into the sauce and simmer for 20 minutes or until the chicken is just cooked – it will continue to cook during stage 3, so don't allow it to overcook now.

Stage 3 is finishing off. Bear in mind that when this bit is done you'll need friends present, rice cooked and some Professor Longhair on the stereo. Heat a little vegetable oil in a small pan and gently fry the onion, green pepper and celery for 2–3 minutes until softened but not coloured. Tip the vegetables into the chicken pot. Stir in the reserved marinade and add the salt and filé powder – this will very slightly thicken the sauce. Finally stir in the remaining ingredients until heated through and serve.

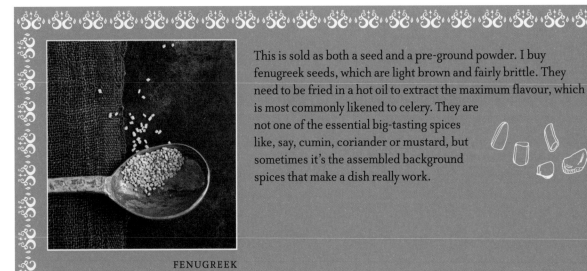

FENUGREEK

This is sold as both a seed and a pre-ground powder. I buy fenugreek seeds, which are light brown and fairly brittle. They need to be fried in a hot oil to extract the maximum flavour, which is most commonly likened to celery. They are not one of the essential big-tasting spices like, say, cumin, coriander or mustard, but sometimes it's the assembled background spices that make a dish really work.

66 My restaurant, The Victoria, recently hosted a special dinner involving several very talented chefs each cooking a course using higher-welfare pork. I was keen to serve something that was very much in the style of our usual menu, and this is the dish that we created for that evening.

Our version for the evening was cooked *à la sous-vide* in a water bath. For those of you who don't practise high-end molecular gastronomy (count me amongst you), a water bath cooks proteins enclosed in a vacuum bag at a very low temperature for a very long time, thus reducing spoilage and other changes that occur when cooking food conventionally. Water baths are very expensive and I'm not about to suggest you invest in one for this recipe. Frankly, we didn't ever use ours enough at the restaurant, so I took it home where my wife now uses it as a foot spa!

The dish itself has mixed parentage, so to speak. The spice mix used is very Sri Lankan in flavour and method, yet later on in the dish a Thai influence comes to bear. When you cast your eyes down the list of ingredients, you may feel a little wary of giving this a go, but I've tried to point out little tips that could make the job easier. A quick heads-up on a couple of ingredients that may seem unfamiliar – kaffir lime leaves are used in many Asian cuisines and they have a wonderful flavour and aroma, and galangal is a member of the ginger family (it looks like a spiky version of ginger) which, when eaten raw, has a more pungent flavour. You should find both of these ingredients in larger supermarkets but also in any good Asian store.

Pork cheeks are boneless nuggets of meat that need a long, slow, cooking, ideal for this sort of curry. I've never seen them in a supermarket, but I have managed to buy them from my butcher. It's worth ordering them a couple of days in advance because he may well not keep them in stock. A large boneless dice of shoulder meat would be a good second option. The Soured Mango 'Noodles' are not essential, but they do give the finished dish a lovely fresh flavour. 99

Braised pork cheeks with coconut & lime leaf served with soured mango 'noodles'

SERVES 4

FOR THE SRI LANKAN-STYLE
CURRY POWDER

1 tablespoon uncooked Basmati rice

3 tablespoons coriander seeds

2 tablespoons cumin seeds

2 tablespoons fennel seeds

7.5cm cinnamon stick

10 green cardamom pods

½ teaspoon black mustard seeds

1½ teaspoons fenugreek seeds

1 teaspoon black peppercorns

3 dried chillies

First make the Sri Lankan-style curry powder. This can be done a few days ahead of the braised pork cheeks, and the quantities given here will provide more than you need, so store what's left in an old spice jar. Heat a frying pan but don't add any oil. Tip in the rice and toast until browned, but don't let it over-colour or it will blacken. Transfer the rice to a plate and set aside to cool. Now do exactly the same with the spices: tip them all into the pan together and dry-roast them until they start to darken slightly. Your kitchen will smell like a tent at the Glastonbury Festival, but don't worry. Transfer the spices to the plate with the rice and allow to cool. Mix the rice and the spices together and grind them to a powder in either an electric spice grinder or using a pestle and mortar.

MORE INGREDIENTS OVERLEAF …   CONTINUED OVERLEAF ⟶

Braised pork cheeks with coconut & lime leaf served with soured mango 'noodles'

CONTINUED FROM PAGE 89

vegetable oil, for frying

12 pork cheeks, trimmed of all fat and sinew

1 onion, finely sliced

2 garlic cloves, finely chopped

5cm piece of fresh galangal, peeled and roughly chopped

1 lemongrass stalk, roughly chopped

3 small hot green chillies, sliced into rings

6 kaffir lime leaves

10 curry leaves

½ teaspoon ground turmeric

½ teaspoon chilli powder

800ml coconut milk

250ml water

juice of 1–2 limes, to taste

2–3 tablespoons liquid palm sugar, to taste

up to 2 tablespoons fish sauce, to taste

Soured Mango 'Noodles' (see page 184), and sticky rice, to serve

To make the braised pork cheeks, heat a casserole pot and pour in a little vegetable oil. Place the pork cheeks into the hot pan and sear until well coloured on all sides. Remove from the pan and set aside. Don't wash out the pan; just add a little more vegetable oil and carry on cooking.

Chuck the onion, garlic, galangal, lemongrass and chillies into the pan. Allow everything to slowly fizz away and caramelise slightly. This should take 10–15 minutes. Add the lime leaves, curry leaves, 2½ teaspoons Sri Lankan-style curry powder, the turmeric and chilli powder and stir. Pour in the coconut milk and the water and return the pork cheeks to the pan. Slowly bring the sauce up to a simmer and cook slowly for 1½ hours.

Fish out a pork cheek and put it on a plate. If the meat is tender enough to cut easily with a spoon, the cheeks are ready. If not, return to the pan and continue to cook for a few minutes longer. Once the cheeks are cooked, remove them all from the sauce and set aside.

Increase the temperature to high and bring the sauce to the boil. Continue to cook until the sauce has reduced a little, then pour through a sieve to remove all the bits. Return the pork cheeks to the sauce and either cool down and refrigerate until required or finish the sauce and serve up.

When you are ready to serve, stir in the lime juice, palm sugar and fish sauce until you feel the taste is just right. Serve each person 3 pork cheeks and pour over some sauce. Place a pile of Soured Mango Noodles on the top of the pork cheeks and serve with plain boiled sticky rice.

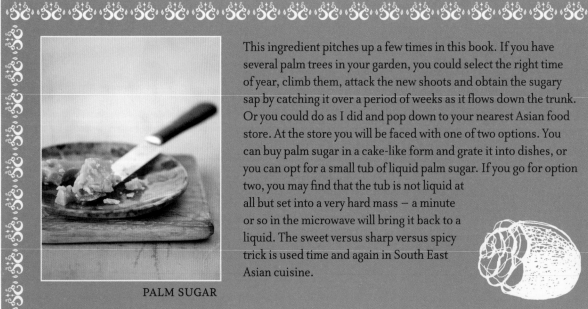

PALM SUGAR

This ingredient pitches up a few times in this book. If you have several palm trees in your garden, you could select the right time of year, climb them, attack the new shoots and obtain the sugary sap by catching it over a period of weeks as it flows down the trunk. Or you could do as I did and pop down to your nearest Asian food store. At the store you will be faced with one of two options. You can buy palm sugar in a cake-like form and grate it into dishes, or you can opt for a small tub of liquid palm sugar. If you go for option two, you may find that the tub is not liquid at all but set into a very hard mass – a minute or so in the microwave will bring it back to a liquid. The sweet versus sharp versus spicy trick is used time and again in South East Asian cuisine.

HOW TO SPATCHCOCK & MARINATE THE QUAIL

'Spatchcock' (an excellent culinary word) describes a butchery technique, which is used to prepare a bird such as a chicken, or indeed a quail, for grilling over coals or in a griddle pan. The backbone is removed so that the bird can be flattened out – thus it's easier to cook. If you buy your meat from a decent butcher, he or she will almost definitely be able to do this for you, but in case they're shut for the day and you have to go to the supermarket, here is what you do. A quail has the same anatomy as a chicken only smaller, so hopefully you'll understand the basic shape and make-up.

Place the bird on a chopping board with the legs pointing towards you. Open up the cavity and you will see the backbone lying flat on the board, running through the middle of the cavity. Poke a sharp knife inside the bird all

the way to the other end. Keep the knife blade to one side of the backbone and cut down along the bone. Repeat this manoeuvre on the other side of the backbone, which should release it completely. Give the bird a push downwards with the palm of your hand and it should remain flat. You have just spatchcocked your first quail! Put your flattened birds in the fridge whilst you prepare the marinade.

For the marinade, squeeze the orange juice into a bowl and add the olive oil, sumac, thyme leaves, honey and ground cumin. Stir everything up. Take the spatchcocked quail and rub them all over with the marinade. Place in a dish, pour over any remaining marinade and leave in the fridge for a couple of hours – overnight would be fine too.

66 Whoever first discovered that quails were good to eat was definitely one very hungry person. A quail is a tiny bird with all its feathers – it's even smaller when you get its kit off. Anyway, that intrepid cook was right: they are tasty little things. The meat is very similar to chicken or guinea fowl and well worth trying if you haven't already.

The celeriac slaw is a bit of an old favourite, turning up from time to time at the restaurant with a variety of dishes. If you are new to the joys of celeriac, imagine a vegetable that looks like a large turnip with a similar density and texture but with a sweet, subtle, celery-type flavour. It is a great partner to the crisp red apple and creamy mayonnaise. The pomegranate dressing not only looks spectacular but also works very well with both the charred meat of the quail and the richness of the slaw. 99

Chargrilled quail with sumac, celeriac & apple slaw & pomegranate dressing

SERVES 4

4 quail, spatchcocked (see left)

juice of 1 orange

100ml olive oil for the marinade, plus a little extra for grilling the quail

2 teaspoons sumac

½ teaspoon thyme leaves

100g honey

2 teaspoons ground cumin

FOR THE CELERIAC & APPLE SLAW

175g chunk of celeriac, finely sliced and then finely shredded into long, thin matchsticks

2 red apples

½ tablespoon grainy mustard

½ tablespoon honey

4–5 tablespoons mayonnaise (yes, a shop-bought one is fine!)

FOR THE POMEGRANATE DRESSING

1 pomegranate

25g caster sugar

50ml olive oil

Spatchcock and marinate the quail – see left. When the time comes to cook the quail, take them out of the fridge and give them a final rub with the marinade before laying, skin-side down on your barbecue or hot griddle pan. Because they are coated with spice and honey the birds will catch and char, but that's good; the burnt skin will add an important flavour to the dish. Give them 4 minutes on the skin side, then flip over and cook on the 'B' side. They may buckle slightly, but just push them down flat again using your tongs. In total your quail will need about 12 minutes.

MAKING THE CELERIAC & APPLE SLAW

Bring a pot of water to the boil and chuck in your very finely shredded celeriac. Give it 1 minute in the boiling water and then pour it into a colander. Tip the hot blanched celeriac into a bowl of cold water to stop the cooking process. Once it's cold, tip it back into the colander and allow it to drain. I sometimes pat it with a clean cloth to make sure all the excess water is removed. Place the drained celeriac into a mixing bowl.

Take the red apples and slice them finely as far as the core. Lay the slices on a chopping board and cut into fine matchsticks. Add this to the celeriac. Mix the grain mustard, honey and mayonnaise and tip this over the celeriac and apple. Mix everything up and keep chilled in the fridge until needed.

THE POMEGRANATE DRESSING

The dressing can be done ahead of time if you are the well-organised type! Cut the pomegranate in half and, after marvelling at how beautiful it is inside, scrape out all the fleshy pips and bung them in a bowl. Squeeze, press and mash the pomegranate to release as much juice as possible. From 1 pomegranate I got about 100ml of juice. Place the juice in a small pan and simmer for 5 minutes with the caster sugar. Remove, cool to room temperature and then whisk in the olive oil. This should result in a rich-red, tangy dressing to trickle over and around the quail with the slaw on the side.

❝ This dish has its roots in Richmond, West London... sort of. It's an irony, but the food most restaurant staff eat is pretty bog standard. I've never worked anywhere where the chefs actually sit down to eat; food is always eaten on the hoof, whilst running around setting up for either lunch or dinner. Chips, pasties, omelettes, baked beans and salads feature heavily.

Curry is without a doubt a favourite with the kitchen staff. We can 'curry up' just about anything. On one joyous occasion, our butcher sent us an extra leg of lamb by mistake. The right and proper course of action would have been to call him and send it back, but where's the fun in that? Instead it was decided that this 'free' gift should be 'curried up' for the boys.

After a bit of research a suitable recipe was found and we set about making this Kashmiri-style curry. We have made it countless times since, each time tweaking the original recipe slightly until we have the perfect curry. This is that very curry, but you don't need six sweaty chefs to make or eat it. We'll pop round by all means, but it's so good that you can safely feed it to your friends, and we have also put it on the menu a few times since.

Kashmir is in the north west of India and can lay claim to many fine culinary inventions, including this one. Our version isn't hot and fiery but is made up of layers of flavour through the use of various aromatic spices. I'd like to thank our butcher for his part in developing this dish. ❞

'Rista' meatballs with saffron & rose water

SERVES 4

1kg boneless lamb, preferably from the leg, diced

1½ tablespoons coriander seeds

1 teaspoon yellow mustard seeds

1 teaspoon cumin seeds

1 teaspoon fenugreek seeds

1½ teaspoons chilli powder

4 garlic cloves, crushed to a paste

25g gram (chickpea) flour

½ teaspoon salt

vegetable oil, for frying

To make the meatballs, the first job is to blend the meat to a fine paste – I know that doesn't sound appealing, but it will be in the end! This is best done in a food-processor. Do the blending in manageable amounts, then put the blended lamb in a bowl in the fridge until needed.

Heat a frying pan and dry-fry the coriander, mustard, cumin and fenugreek seeds until they start to brown very slightly. Leave to cool, then grind to a fine powder in a pestle and mortar.

Take the lamb out of the fridge and add the freshly ground spice mixture along with the chilli powder, garlic, gram flour and salt. Mix well to combine and then roll the seasoned meat into balls about the size of a golf ball using your hands. The mixture should make about 16 meatballs. Heat a frying pan and add a little vegetable oil. Fry the meatballs in batches until they are a rich brown colour all over and then pop them onto a plate to one side (they shouldn't be cooked through at this stage).

Now find a pot to cook the curry. Heat it over a medium heat and add a little vegetable oil. Tip in the onions, garlic and ginger and cook for 20 minutes or more over a medium heat until they are a dark brown colour. Don't rush this stage or the ingredients will burn – remember, dark brown, not black! If they catch on the bottom or the sides of the pan, add a tablespoon of water and stir vigorously to work the caught bits back in to the bulk. This caramelisation adds an important element to the finished flavour.

FOR THE SAUCE

vegetable oil, for frying

2 onions, finely chopped

5 garlic cloves, finely chopped

70g fresh ginger, peeled and grated

125ml natural yogurt

5 cloves

4 cardamom pods

12.5cm cinnamon stick, broken into 3

4 teaspoons chilli flakes

1 teaspoon asafoetida

1 teaspoon ground ginger

1.6 litres water

125g dried green lentils

½ teaspoon salt

good pinch of saffron

3 teaspoons rose water

Add the yogurt, cloves, cardamom, cinnamon, chilli, asafoetida and ground ginger. Continue to cook until the yogurt is completely reduced and almost dry. Pour in the water and add the lentils. Bring to a simmer and cook for a further 10 minutes.

Tip in the coloured meatballs and the salt. Reduce the heat and cook slowly for 40 minutes or until the meatballs are cooked through and the lentils are soft and breaking up slightly. Remove the meatballs from the sauce and set aside. Blend the sauce very roughly using a stick blender to allow the lentils to thicken it slightly, but don't overdo it as the sauce should have plenty of texture. Return the meatballs to the pan and stir in the saffron and rose water just before serving. Kashmir is a traditional rice-growing region, so a bowl of Basmati is the very best thing to serve with this.

The first thing to point out is that asafoetida bloody stinks. Don't throw yours away, thinking it's off – they sold it to you like that! Luckily that smell does not convert taste-wise during cooking. It's available either as a lump that needs grinding, or in powder form. I add a pinch or two to meat skewers, dhal and various curries. The flavour it imparts is similar to that of onion powder. Interestingly I've just read that it is known for counteracting flatulence (must send my dad some for Christmas).

ASAFOETIDA

> This is an old favourite both at home and at the restaurant. I've suggested using lamb rump because it's one of my preferred cuts, but you could use a rack of lamb, loin or even a shoulder. The salsa is really simple and can be made in advance and served up at room temperature, and the baba ghanoush is also best made well before required, so all in all the work involved just before serving is minimal, making this a great dinner-party dish. Dhana jeera can be bought in specialist spice shops, but don't bother as you can easily make your own by roasting and grinding cumin and coriander seeds. As this dish is really an assembly of small elements, I've divided the recipe up into stages with suggestions on when to cook what.

Dhana jeera spiced lamb rump with sweet potato, baba ghanoush & aubergine salsa

SERVES 4

3 tablespoons coriander seeds

2 tablespoons cumin seeds

100ml olive oil

4 square-cut lamb rumps, each about 175g (ask your butcher and they will know what you want!)

vegetable oil, for frying

1 quantity Baba Ghanoush (see page 182), to serve

FOR THE AUBERGINE SALSA

350ml olive oil

1 aubergine, cut into 1cm dice

4 garlic cloves, crushed to a paste

50g fresh coriander, shredded

grated zest and juice of 1 lime

4 red chillies, finely chopped

FOR THE SWEET POTATOES

4 sweet potatoes, peeled and cut into 3cm dice

olive oil, for frying

pinch of salt (optional)

MAKING THE DHANA JEERA AND MARINATING THE LAMB

This job is best done the day before you intend to eat the dish. Dry-fry the coriander and cumin seeds in a hot frying pan until they start to change colour. They will smoke a bit and smell fantastic. Set the seeds aside to cool, then grind them to as fine a powder as you can using a spice grinder or a pestle and mortar. You will need 4 teaspoons for this recipe and the remainder can be stored in an old spice jar.

To marinate the lamb, whisk together 4 teaspoons of dhana jeera with the olive oil in a bowl to form a paste. Place the lamb in the bowl and rub thoroughly with the spice paste. Chill in the fridge until required.

MAKING THE SALSA

Make the salsa up to 2 hours before serving. Heat a wok and pour in the olive oil. When the oil is nice and hot, tip in the aubergine and fry it until it turns a light golden-brown colour. Transfer the aubergine to a colander placed over a bowl to catch the oil. Set the oil aside and allow to cool completely.

Put the aubergine into another bowl and add the garlic, fresh coriander, lime zest and juice and chillies. When the oil is cool, pour it into the bowl containing the aubergine and stir everything up well. Leave to stand at room temperature.

PREPARING THE SWEET POTATOES

Boil the sweet potatoes in a pan of water until just tender. Drain and leave to cool, then chill until required (this could be done up to a day in advance).

TURNING ALL OF THAT LOT INTO THE DISH ITSELF!

Your friends have arrived, they are tucking in to your best wine and they are building up an appetite, so ...

Preheat the oven to 175°C/gas mark 4. Heat a small frying pan over a medium heat and add a little vegetable oil.

Fry the spiced lamb rumps in the pan until roasty brown all over. Transfer them to the oven and cook for about 12 minutes until cooked to medium.

Heat a good splash of olive oil in a separate, larger frying pan and add the sweet potatoes. Fry until browned all over and beginning to caramelise – this gives them a fabulous taste. Add a pinch of salt, if liked.

Place a pile of potatoes into each person's bowl, halve each lamb rump and pop that on top of the sweet potato. Spoon over some aubergine salsa and dollop on some Baba Ghanoush.

Sorted!

97

66 My business partner Greg gave me a barbecue for my birthday last year. He's a Kiwi, which means he is genetically programmed to barbecue at a moment's notice. I, on the other hand, have never been overly keen on barbecues. For me the kitchen offers so much more scope and control when cooking, and I'd always noted that whenever I was invited to a friend's barbecue the cooking would be done by the partner who was normally only allowed to pour and serve drinks at a regular dinner party (amongst my friends that normally means the male half of the team). Men like to cook, but only if there is a suitably adoring audience. They don't go for the mundane budget-controlled cookery that takes place from Monday to Thursday, but give them a barbecue and a crowd, and all of a sudden they're experts at cooking everything from pork chops to king prawns. Or so they think.

I believe one of the big mistakes when having a barbecue is the tendency to feel that you must cook such a wide range of meats – this inevitably means that everyone eats their meal in tiny stages as the next wave of chops, sausages or skewers comes off the hot coals. My advice is to pick one decent cut of meat and cook it beautifully. Here is one such meat. A whole leg of lamb is perfect for the charcoal because the outside will benefit from the high heat and flames whilst the centre of the meat stays pink and sweet. I would suggest (and not merely for self-marketing purposes) that you serve this with Roasted Vegetable Couscous (see page 108) and a bowl of Tzatziki (see page 182). 99

BUTTERFLYING A LEG OF LAMB

I suggest seeking your butcher's assistance with the lamb. Ask him or her to remove the bone completely and to cut open the leg so that it becomes a large, boneless, flat piece of meat. This style of preparation is called 'butterflying' and the resulting piece of lamb will cook relatively quickly, and will also be very easy to carve.

Barbecued marinated leg of lamb

A DECENT-SIZED LEG SHOULD EASILY FEED 6–8 HUNGRY FRIENDS

1 leg of lamb, about 2.5kg on the bone
  or 1.5kg boned, boned and
  butterflied (explanation opposite!)

FOR THE MARINADE

1 glass red wine

4 star anise

2 cinnamon sticks

4 cloves

1 tablespoon coriander seeds

250ml medium sherry

1 orange, cut into 8 thick slices

2 heads of garlic, quartered

sprig of rosemary

1 tablespoon demerara sugar

100ml olive oil

The marinade needs to hit the lamb at least 24 hours prior to lift-off, so the day before your barbecue pour the wine into a small pan and bring to a simmer. Chuck in the star anise, cinnamon, cloves and coriander seeds (the heat of the wine will bring out the flavours of the spices a little more than if you just make a raw, cold marinade). Simmer for a minute or two, then remove from the heat and set aside to cool completely.

Pour the wine and spices into a bowl and add the sherry, orange slices, garlic, rosemary, sugar and oil. This is the marinade ready to go. Lay the lamb in a large baking tray and pour over the marinade. It should cover the lamb but if it doesn't quite, you may need to turn the meat over occasionally. Leave to marinate in the fridge for 24 hours.

About an hour before cooking the lamb, remove it from the marinade and pick off any of the bits that may have stuck to the meat. Preheat the barbecue and place the lamb over very hot coals (about 10cm from the surface of the coals). Let it sizzle away undisturbed for 5–6 minutes so that it really starts to colour up. Turn it over and do the same on the other side, then, if your barbecue allows, lift the rack to increase the distance between coals and meat to about 20cm. This will reduce the risk of burning the meat. The total cooking time will very much depend on the size of the leg, but should be around 45 minutes – I would turn it over at least twice more during this time. If you are lucky enough to own a food thermometer, take your lamb off the barbecue when the core temperature reaches 55–60°C.

A large chunk of meat like this should ideally be allowed to rest before being carved and eaten. That way the muscle relaxes, meaning the juices are kept within the meat rather than pouring out all over the chopping board, or worse, your best friend's wife's lap.

Apparently the UK's Guild of Food Writers has nearly 400 authors, journalists and columnists on its books. I'm not one of them. I had half hoped that one day I would get the old tap-on-the-shoulder and be taken off to an oak-panelled room, deep below a private members' club in Shaftesbury Avenue, where I would be secretly inducted into this society after undergoing various exotic (culinary-based) rituals. Well, not any more. I am about to deliver my ambitions a fatal blow... I am listing amongst the ingredients for this dish a 'meat curry ready meal'(!). It's a shameful ingredient but one I can justify, even if it does mean that I will never again be commissioned to write a cookery book.

This is one of my favourite dishes in the world. It's a simple mix of fresh ingredients, stir-fried with chopped bread, meat curry and egg. Kottu roti is a very popular dish in Sri Lanka, often sold as street food. As well as the amazing aroma and the incredible taste, it's also the *sound* of kottu roti that is so memorable. The dish is traditionally cooked on a flat hotplate or griddle and the ingredients are manoeuvred and chopped with large blades similar to those used by a baker to cut dough. The guys have a blade in either hand and they chop, chop, chop the ingredients as they are cooking. Each vendor appears to have a slightly different rhythm and style and the sound is hypnotic. If you type 'kottu roti' into a search engine, you'll see videos of these guys at work. Gil Scott-Heron would have given anything for a percussionist with their flare!

The actual cooking of kottu roti is relatively simple but the problem is that the list of ingredients in most recipes includes items that need cooking before they can be listed as ingredients, if you see what I mean. The roti bread used is called *gothamba* and most recipes seem to assume that you will have a pile of this stuff lying around! And then halfway through they order you to add your cold meat curry, which is a complete recipe in itself. My aim is to try to find a quicker, simpler way of getting you to give this dish a go. Therefore, at the risk of jeopardising my career, I'm suggesting that you purchase a different yet useable bread for this dish and that you either use up a leftover meat curry or simply buy a ready-made one. If this works and you love it, then please look up a genuine kottu recipe, make your own gothamba roti, buy the blades and griddle plate and get chopping for real.

Meat kottu roti

SERVES 4

CURRY NOTE

You can use any type of meat curry here. The Basic Curry (see page 126) could be made specifically for this dish or (better still) use leftover curry, or buy a ready-made curry, but in all cases bear in mind the weight given here is for the meat only and you should remove the meat from any gravy or sauce before using.

CONTINUED... ⟶

Meat kottu roti

CONTINUED FROM PAGE 100

2 tablespoons vegetable oil

1 large onion, chopped

3 garlic cloves, chopped

40g fresh ginger, peeled and grated

50 curry leaves

2 green bird's eye chillies, finely sliced

4 spring onions, shredded

2 medium carrots, grated

1½ teaspoons cumin seeds

1½ teaspoons black mustard seeds

1 teaspoon salt

6 ready-made roti or paratha cut
    into 5mm x 5cm strips

450g ready-made meat curry
    (see Curry Note on page 100)

4 eggs, beaten

shredded iceberg lettuce, to garnish

I don't have a griddle plate at home, so I use a wok to make kottu roti, and I shall assume that you too are more likely to have a wok than a full-on griddle set up in your kitchen. You will also need a large metal kitchen spoon to use for chopping and stir-frying. The following cooking process will take about 8 minutes in total. Fast food!

Heat a wok on the largest ring of your hob. We need to have a good high heat throughout this process. Pour in 1 tablespoon of the vegetable oil and get it really hot. Tip in and fry the onion, garlic, ginger, curry leaves, chillies, spring onions and carrots – use your spoon to move the bits about in the wok. A little colour is a good thing at this point. Stir in the cumin and mustard seeds and the salt. Add the remaining oil and chuck in the strips of roti or paratha along with the meat curry.

Chop and stir, ensuring that everything comes into contact with the hot wok in order to heat through properly. Continue to chop and stir and try to find your natural rhythm – we are talking upbeat and funky, not a mournful ballad! Pour in the eggs and chop and stir these through as well. As they cook, the eggs will give a springy texture to the dish.

It's ready! Portion into bowls, sprinkle over the lettuce and serve.

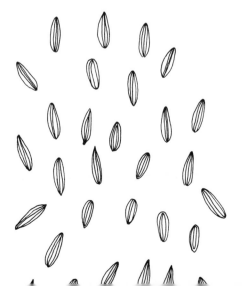

CURRY LEAF

This is one of my favourite ingredients, but first things first. Curry leaf is not what is used to make curry powder. Yes, it is used in curries, but that's different. Curry leaf comes from a small tree. The leaves are sold in clusters attached to a main stem. They can be dried or frozen but are always better fresh. You can scrunch them up and add them to your cooking, but the best extraction of flavour is through frying them. I have seen the use of curry leaf in Asian cuisine likened to that of bay leaf in European cuisine, but I feel that's doing it an injustice. I've regularly tossed bay leaves into stews and sauces and wondered if they make any real difference at all, but curry leaf has an incredible flavour that's instantly recognisable.

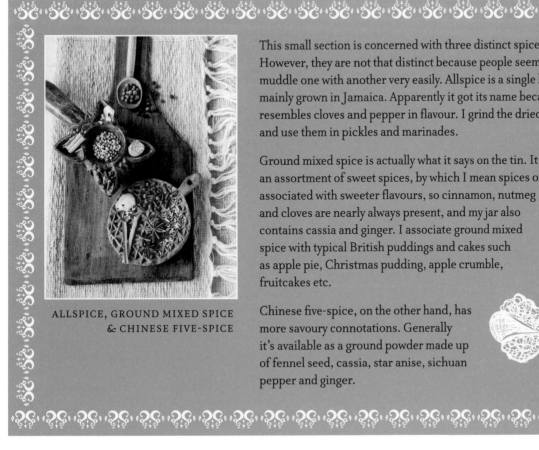

ALLSPICE, GROUND MIXED SPICE & CHINESE FIVE-SPICE

This small section is concerned with three distinct spices. However, they are not that distinct because people seem to muddle one with another very easily. Allspice is a single berry mainly grown in Jamaica. Apparently it got its name because it resembles cloves and pepper in flavour. I grind the dried berries and use them in pickles and marinades.

Ground mixed spice is actually what it says on the tin. It's an assortment of sweet spices, by which I mean spices often associated with sweeter flavours, so cinnamon, nutmeg and cloves are nearly always present, and my jar also contains cassia and ginger. I associate ground mixed spice with typical British puddings and cakes such as apple pie, Christmas pudding, apple crumble, fruitcakes etc.

Chinese five-spice, on the other hand, has more savoury connotations. Generally it's available as a ground powder made up of fennel seed, cassia, star anise, sichuan pepper and ginger.

I love a rare rib-eye steak as much as the next man, but nothing can beat beef that has been slowly braised in a carefully balanced stock. The French, of course, are masters of this style of cooking and at the restaurant we will often braise short ribs with red wine, garlic and thyme and then serve them with wild mushrooms and bone marrow. But for a very different take, try this recipe – it's a meat eater's delight: a very large chunk of tender beef on the bone packed with Asian flavours. Although the cooking time is lengthy, the actual work involved is minimal.

Asian spiced short ribs

SERVES 4

vegetable oil, for frying

4 short beef ribs, each weighing about 550g

8 garlic cloves, roughly chopped

6 green bird's eye chillies, roughly chopped

150g fresh ginger, peeled and roughly sliced

1½ tablespoons Chinese five-spice powder

5 star anise, bashed up a little in a pestle and mortar

1 teaspoon salt

75g demerara sugar

5 tablespoons soy sauce

1 tablespoon fish sauce

1 tablespoon red wine vinegar

juice of 1 orange

about 3 litres beef stock

5 lemongrass stalks, bruised and frayed

TO SERVE

12 long sprigs of coriander, stored in cold water in the fridge

4 spring onions, finely sliced on the diagonal

4 red chillies, finely sliced on the diagonal

sticky white rice

It's well worth assembling all the ingredients, except for the last three items, before you begin cooking so that you are completely ready.

First, colour the short ribs. At this stage you are not trying to cook them at all, just to build up a good caramelisation all over. Heat a splash of vegetable oil in a frying pan. Place 2 of the ribs into the pan and cook, turning once, until coloured on both sides. Remove from the pan. Repeat with the remaining 2 ribs and set aside.

Heat another splash of vegetable oil in a casserole pot or pan large enough to hold the ribs comfortably. Chuck in the garlic, chillies and ginger and fry for a minute or two. A small amount of colour is okay – not too much! Add the Chinese five-spice powder along with the star anise, salt and sugar, and give this all a good stir. Add the soy sauce, fish sauce, red wine vinegar and orange juice – this should immediately seethe – and boil for a minute.

Pour over the beef stock and add the lemongrass. Carefully place the ribs into the pan – they need to be submerged in stock, so push them to the bottom and add a dash of water if they're still poking above the surface. Reduce the heat to low so that the stock doesn't even simmer (this is very important as if you cook the meat in boiling stock it will tighten and force out the natural juices, leaving you with a great stock but dry meat). Leave to cook for 1½–2 hours or until the meat is really tender. If the level of stock falls well below the beef, top it up with a little water.

Transfer the ribs to a plate to cool. Strain the stock to remove all the bits and return to the pan. Bring to a rapid boil and cook until reduced by half to form a very rich, spicy and highly aromatic broth, as it shall now be known (because it sounds more Asian and a lot more appealing!). Cool and chill until required if not using straight away.

Return the beef to the pan with the boiling broth to warm up. The beef probably won't be submerged in the broth, but that's okay – use tongs to turn the ribs over until they are heated through and nice and tender.

If by chance it's summer and you have a barbecue available, you could reheat the cooked short ribs over charcoal and then pour over the broth – this would add a wonderful smoky flavour.

Place the beef onto a large serving dish and pour over the broth. Drain the coriander and scatter over the beef, along with the spring onions and chillies. Serve with plain sticky white rice.

A WORD ON SHORT RIBS

Often called Jacob's ladder, short ribs are made up of four or five 25cm sections of rib bone with a large chunk of meat in between. They are big and bulky, but require little in the way of preparation, apart from cutting into portions. To do this, cut through the middle of the meat that separates the bone so that you end up with a single strip of meat and bone. Bear in mind that the bone is heavy, so you'll need to factor that in when deciding how much to buy. For my four portions here I started with a single four-bone piece weighing 2.2kg. I then cut this into four fairly evenly sized pieces. Any butcher will know what you are after, but some may need a day or two to get it in, so it's worth pre-ordering if you can.

A WORD ON BEEF STOCK

In a professional kitchen beef stock is produced each week as a matter of course. At home, of course, this usually isn't an option, so I tend to use a decent fresh ready-made beef stock. I have on occasions just used beef stock cubes and, to be honest, with all the other flavours involved they work just as well.

Okay, you don't have to eat these for supper – in fact some are just as good for lunch – it's just that publishers love a catchy title! I love cooking, but sometimes on a grey and wet Wednesday night, inspiration (and time) are a little hard to come by, so the dishes in this chapter will, I hope, provide you with a few ideas that can be knocked up fairly simply without costing a fortune.

Quick & simple
supper spice

66 It's a few pages now since I've had a rant, so I thought one was due... Cooking on telly can be problematic at times. This dish is a case in point. I cooked it on a morning cookery show on which I was a guest chef. Programme makers are very keen to cover all bases and they are forever asking for alternative ingredients and options on the chosen dish.

The process begins with a phone call inviting you on to the show...

'Hi, is that Matt Tebbut?'

'No, it's Paul Merrett.'

'So sorry, Paul, my mistake – Matt's busy and we have you down as a backup.'

'Great... thanks.'

'We'd like to get you on the show. The topic is summer food and you can cook whatever you want...'

'Cool. I'll do a slow-baked shoulder of lamb – ideal for the barbecue.'

'No lamb, I'm afraid. Allegra did that two weeks ago.'

'Hmm, did she. I know – paella.'

'Exec. producer says we can't do any more rice dishes on the show.'

'Okay, what about a whole stuffed sea bass with roasted fennel and aioli?'

'That sounds a bit tricky for the average viewer. Some are not that adventurous... can you make a nice salad?'

'They have chosen to watch a sodding cookery programme to be fair... but okay, what about a roasted vegetable couscous salad with feta and pomegranate?'

'Oh, perfect – that sounds fantastic. One thing, could you swap the feta for Cheddar in case that's all they have in the fridge?'

'Well, you could, but it wouldn't be the same. Can't they whizz out and buy some feta?'

'And what about the pomegranate. Could that be exchanged for anything?'

'Look, you could make it with bloody Mini Babybell and tinned mandarins if you want, but this version works best.'

And I'm right, this version does work best. It's a really simple supper, which you can customise any way you wish, but this is how it works best. You could make this dish well ahead of time – possibly even the day before – but for best results serve at room temperature, never from the fridge. There are many ways to cook couscous. If you live next door to a North African who has given you her great grandmother's method, use that. If not, mine will work fine. Lastly, a quick word on the vegetables. The recipe title has 'roasted' vegetables, but we aren't going to roast them at all – we are going to cook them in a frying pan on the hob. Menu and recipe writers are allowed a little artistic licence! 99

Roasted vegetable couscous with feta & pomegranate

SERVES 4 AS A MAIN COURSE — A SIDE SALAD WOULD BE NICE BUT NO NEED FOR MUCH ELSE

CONTINUED... ───────────▶

Roasted vegetable couscous with feta & pomegranate

CONTINUED FROM PAGE 108

FOR THE COUSCOUS

250g couscous

90ml extra-virgin olive oil

1 teaspoon fennel seeds

2 teaspoons ras-el-hanout

1 teaspoon cumin seeds

1 teaspoon ground turmeric

½ teaspoon chilli flakes

⅔ teaspoon salt

3 garlic cloves, chopped

180ml boiling water

FOR THE 'ROASTED' VEGETABLES

about 200ml extra-virgin olive oil

1 small aubergine, cut into wedges

1 red onion, cut into wedges

1 red pepper, cut into large dice

1 yellow pepper, cut into large dice

1 head broccoli, cut into small florets

1 small sweet potato, peeled and diced

6 button mushrooms, sliced

TO SERVE

3 plum tomatoes, cut into chunky dice

200g feta cheese, broken into chunks

25g coriander, chopped

5 mint leaves, chopped

1 pomegranate

300ml extra-virgin olive oil

Tip the couscous into a bowl. Heat the oil in a frying pan until hot but not smoking. Add the spices, salt and garlic and leave to fizz and splutter for 2 minutes, then tip into the bowl with the couscous and mix well. The heat will bring out the flavour of the spices whilst the oil will help prevent the couscous from clumping up into lumps. Pour the boiling water over the couscous, stir and immediately cover tightly with clingfilm. Set aside for 8–10 minutes.

Now for the 'roasted' vegetables … all of which should be cooked over a medium–high heat until they are just cooked.

AUBERGINE

Heat 70ml of the oil in a frying pan and fry the aubergine until dark brown and cooked through (7–8 minutes). Transfer to a plate and set aside.

RED ONION

Pour another 30ml of the oil into the frying pan and fry the onion until golden brown and softened (3–4 minutes). Tip onto the same plate as the aubergine.

PEPPERS

Add 20ml more of the oil to the frying pan and fry the peppers until slightly softened and begining to caramelise (2–3 minutes). Transfer to the plate.

BROCCOLI

Heat 30ml of the oil and cook the broccoli until lightly charred – be brave and let it catch and colour (2 minutes). Tip onto the cooked veg plate.

SWEET POTATO

Pan-fry, using about 30ml more of the oil, until caramelised and soft (5–6 minutes), then remove to the plate.

BUTTON MUSHROOMS

Heat the remaining 20ml oil and fry until caramelised and soft (3–4 minutes), then tip onto the cooked veg plate.

Tip all of the vegetables into the bowl with the couscous. Fluff up the couscous using a fork, which will also mix in the veg.

To serve, add the tomatoes, feta and herbs to the couscous and mix through. Halve the pomegranate and use a spoon to scoop out the flesh, including any juice, and add to the couscous. Pour in the olive oil and give the whole thing a final mix. A side salad and yogurt dip go well with couscous – the Mint & Mango Yogurt Dip on page 192 would be a winner.

Found throughout Algeria, Tunisia and Morocco, ras-el-hanout is not a single spice but a blend of many – sometimes up to 30 spices are used. To complicate matters further, the spices within ras-el-hanout are not set in stone. Each spice seller will pick the very best spices for his own batch. Ras-el-hanout means 'top-of-the-shop', so expect a slightly different flavour with every batch you buy! However, for my simple Storecupboard Ras-el-hanout, see page 119.

RAS-EL-HANOUT

> My first ever job (way, way back!) was as an apprentice chef at The Ritz London. One of my daily tasks was to make and shape the falafel mix, so popular with the Middle Eastern guests. Prior to this I had never heard of falafel – this was years before it became the über-trendy food of choice from Notting Hill to Camden Market.
>
> Falafel are small, highly flavoured, fried nuggets of ground raw chickpeas. They are popular throughout the Middle East, although the actual falafel epicentre is shrouded in mystery. An Egyptian taxi driver kindly informed me that falafel originated in Egypt, whilst a Lebanese barber was adamant that they were actually first served in Lebanon. Get the picture?
>
> Anyway, I love falafel and I wanted to include a recipe in this book. The problem is I feel a bit mean encouraging you to make these crispy fritters without advising you on ways to use them. The good news is that falafel production can take place on a large scale as they freeze well and can be fried straight from frozen. So here are three falafelly suggestions. (Yes, three! That's three FREE recipes when you think about it – you won't get that in your average cookbook!) I reckon this will keep you happily eating falafel for weeks to come.

Reasons to make falafel 1, 2 & 3

FOR THE BASIC FALAFEL MIXTURE

400g dried chickpeas (never use canned chickpeas as you need the absorption quality of the dried)

60g chopped fresh coriander

120g fresh ginger, grated

4 red chillies, finely chopped

2 garlic cloves, finely chopped

8 spring onions, roughly chopped

good pinch of salt

vegetable oil, for deep-frying

Soak the chickpeas for 6 hours or overnight. Drain and tip into the bowl of a blender or food-processor. Add the remaining ingredients and whizz until the mixture resembles breadcrumbs. (Don't blend to a smooth paste as that will inhibit the finished texture.) Shape the falafel according to your chosen recipe (see below). The falafel can be either frozen or fried straight away.

GENERAL FALAFEL-FRYING TIPS

To fry from fresh or frozen, half fill a large, high-sided pan with oil and heat to 175°C. Fry the falafel until deep golden brown in colour, carefully remove from the oil using a slotted spoon, drain on kitchen paper and proceed with your chosen recipe below.

The three reasons

1. FALAFEL BURGERS

These can be shaped by hand; however, I push the mixture inside a pastry cutter to form a perfect burger shape. Fry and serve in a sesame bun with tomato, lettuce and Tzatziki (see page 182).

2. FALAFEL SALAD

Overfill a dessert spoon with falafel mixture. Press the spoon against your palm to form the falafel into a sort of egg shape. Fry and serve warm with a salad involving roasted pepper and aubergine, feta cheese and tomato.

3. FALAFEL WRAP

Roll the falafel mixture into a walnut-sized ball. Fry, then arrange in the centre of a tortilla wrap. Top with a little Greek yogurt, finely sliced red onion, grated Cheddar cheese and shredded lettuce.

❝ Okay, to you and me this is really a cheese toastie, but, let's face it, quesadilla does sound a lot more exotic! To the professional caterer, that means we can put the price up by at least a quid or two, and for home cooks it means you can serve it to friends without them calling you a cheapskate. A lot of my quesadilla consumption actually takes place between meals as they make a great afternoon snack (not bad as an after-pub snack, too).

The word 'quesadilla' comes from the Spanish for cheese. It's actually Mexican in origin and, as well as cheese, the other essential ingredient is the flour tortillas, or wraps as they are sometimes called. Beyond that, the world of quesadillas is open to interpretation… ❞

Tomato & spring onion quesadilla with three bean, chilli & avocado salsa

SERVES 4

8 flour tortillas or wraps

200g Cheddar cheese, grated

4 large tomatoes, thinly sliced

1 bunch of spring onions, finely sliced

2 tablespoons olive oil

FOR THE SALSA

200g canned cannellini beans,
    rinsed and drained

200g canned kidney beans, rinsed
    and drained

200g canned chickpeas, rinsed
    and drained

½ red onion, finely chopped

2 red chillies, finely diced

1 ripe avocado, peeled, stoned
    and diced

2 tablespoons olive oil

dash of balsamic vinegar

juice of ½ lemon

Lay 4 of the tortillas or wraps onto the work surface and sprinkle with half of the cheese. Layer the tomatoes on top to cover as much of the tortillas as possible. Sprinkle over the spring onions and top with the remaining cheese. Place the 4 remaining tortillas on top to form 4 round sandwiches. It's worth mentioning that the cheese glues the wraps together, which is why we put it top and bottom.

Heat ½ a tablespoon of the oil in a frying pan large enough to hold a quesadilla. Lay one in the pan and leave to sizzle for about 2 minutes or until crisp and brown. And now comes the only dramatic moment in quesadilla production – you need to flip it over! The easiest way of doing this is to put a palette knife underneath and your hand on the cool top and gently turn it over. Cook on the 'B' side for a further 2 minutes, then slide out of the pan onto a plate. Repeat with the remaining 3 quesadillas.

To make the salsa, mix the beans and chickpeas together in a bowl and add the onion, chillies and avocado. Pour in the olive oil, balsamic vinegar and lemon juice. Scatter this over the quesadillas and serve.

" This dish, of course, doesn't have to be frozen – feel free to make the dhal and eat it right there and then – but it can be made in a large batch and put in the freezer, so that you are only a quick ping in the microwave away from a very simple supper. Dhal is a dish eaten all over India, with various regional twists. There is a wide variety of pulses that you could use instead of red lentils: chickpeas, green lentils and yellow split peas all work very well. Dhal like this can be eaten as is, with a simple salad and some flatbread, or you could serve it with a curry.

Paneer is commonly used in Indian cuisine, and most of us probably first encounter it in 'matar paneer', which pleasingly translates as cheesy peas. The first time I made matar paneer, the only option was to make the cheese myself, but it is now stocked in most supermarkets. If you do fancy a bit of cheese production, see the paneer recipe on page 201. "

Red lentil dhal for the freezer

MAKES 2 LITRES OF DHAL, WHICH I RECKON IS ABOUT 12 MAIN-COURSE PORTIONS

vegetable oil, for frying

3 onions, finely chopped

4 garlic cloves, finely chopped

7.5cm piece of fresh ginger, peeled and grated

4 red chillies, finely chopped

½ tablespoon chilli powder

2 teaspoons asafoetida

1 teaspoon yellow mustard seeds

½ tablespoon ground turmeric

½ tablespoon ground cumin

½ tablespoon cumin seeds

1 tablespoon ground coriander

1½ tablespoons curry powder

1 tablespoon garam masala

1kg dried red lentils, rinsed and drained

½ teaspoon salt

400ml can coconut milk

TO SERVE

vegetable oil, for frying

3 sweet potatoes, peeled and diced

400g paneer

300g frozen peas, defrosted

good handful of spinach

2 tablespoons chopped fresh coriander

Heat the oil in a large pan and fry the onions, garlic, ginger and chillies until golden brown. Tip in the spices and lentils, stir and leave everything to sizzle a bit.

Pour over about 2 litres water to cover the lentils, then add the salt and coconut milk.

Bring to a simmer and cook until the lentils are soft and much of the liquid has been absorbed. There are not hard-and-fast rules here – you are in charge. I like my dhal to be the consistency of Greek yogurt, while my mum's dhal is much thinner, almost sauce-like.

Right, more decisions ... At the moment your dhal is very textured because most of the lentils will have swollen and broken. I like this texture, but if you prefer a smooth dhal, grab your stick blender and purée the contents of the pan. Either way, the dhal is now ready for the freezer.

If you're not freezing it, or if you have defrosted dhal at the ready, here's how to finish it off prior to serving. Warm it in a pan or the microwave. Meanwhile, heat a little oil in a pan and fry the sweet potatoes until caramelised and cooked through. Tip into the dhal.

Dice or break up the paneer and fry with a touch of oil until coloured on all sides, then add to the dhal. Chuck in the peas, spinach and fresh coriander. Stir to warm through and serve.

66 A short while ago I was asked what would be my desert island dish, and biriyani got the nod. Every two weeks or so I make the short trip to Southall near my home in London for some real Indian food, and I have to force myself to try new dishes rather than order what I really want – a biriyani! In case you don't know, a biriyani is a fragrant concoction of scented rice to which one can add seafood, chicken or mutton or, as is the case here, keep it vegetarian.

The art of making a good, genuine biriyani can be very complex both in terms of ingredients and method. I certainly encourage you to experiment, but everyone needs a starting point and this is a simple stove-top, weekday supper version that won't challenge your cookery skills to the limit. A word about rice quantities: most recipes generally recommend 50g per serving, but in my house that's never enough, so I've upped it to 75g – you won't regret having more! 99

After-work stove-top biriyani

SERVES 4

300g Basmati rice

3 tablespoons vegetable oil

1 large onion, finely sliced

12 button mushrooms, sliced

3 garlic cloves, finely chopped

60g fresh ginger, peeled and grated

2 plum tomatoes, finely chopped

2.5cm cinnamon stick

½ teaspoon fennel seeds

½ teaspoon cumin seeds

20 curry leaves

1 tablespoon hot curry powder

½ teaspoon salt

150g frozen peas

400g broccoli, broken into
small florets

1 tablespoon chopped fresh coriander

Rinse the rice in a sieve under cold running water, drain thoroughly and set aside.

Heat the oil in a flameproof, lidded casserole pot roughly 25cm in diameter and 10cm deep. Chuck in the onion and mushrooms and fry for 5 minutes or until slightly coloured. Add the garlic, ginger and tomatoes and leave to sizzle for 2 minutes or until the moisture from the tomatoes has evaporated. Add the cinnamon, fennel seeds, cumin seeds, curry leaves and curry powder and cook for a minute or so. Tip in the rice and salt and very gently stir to mix everything up a little. (Stirring rice causes the grains to release starch, which makes for a gluey, sticky supper, so go carefully. See page 200 for more on cooking rice).

Now you need to add cold water – I haven't given a measurement here because I was taught to cook rice by an elderly Bangladeshi cook and he had an ingenious method. Fill a measuring jug with cold water; gently pour it into the casserole pot until it just covers the rice. At this point, put your index finger into the pot (trust me!) with the tip touching the rice, and pour in more water until it reaches the first joint of your finger. This may seem mad but it works – every time! Bring to a rapid boil. (I didn't mention removing your finger because I guessed you'd realise that!)

Tip in the peas and broccoli but don't stir. Bring back to the boil. Cover the casserole pot with foil and the lid to trap the steam. Cook for exactly 5 minutes, then switch off the heat and leave well alone for 20 minutes. Don't be tempted to lift the lid or the steam will escape.

After 20 minutes, lift the lid off your perfectly cooked biriyani, fluff up the rice, sprinkle over the coriander and serve.

66 A Moroccan tagine is a slow-cooked stew, named after the clay pot in which it's cooked. This recipe is possibly not as Moroccan as most – it's my make-it-quick-at-home version – so if you don't own a tagine, don't worry, I won't say a word. I have purposely tried to keep the ingredients limited and familiar because it seems wrong to boast that you can cook this in 25 minutes if it takes 3 days to track down authentic yet curious ingredients, such as pigeon, agarwood or fresh quince.

One spice that you will see mentioned in many tagine recipes is ras-el-hanout, which is actually not one spice at all but a selection of the finest spices a particular supplier has to offer. It is available online, but you will likely have many of the spices contained within sitting in your storecupboard right now. 99

Twenty-five-minute (or thereabouts) vegetable tagine with cauliflower couscous

SERVES 4

200ml olive oil

500g sweet potato, peeled and cut into chunky dice

500g new potatoes, thickly sliced

1 yellow pepper, diced

1 red pepper, diced

1 large red onion, cut into 12 wedges

8 garlic cloves, roughly chopped

400g can chopped tomatoes

pinch of salt

20 pitted green olives

400g can chickpeas, rinsed and drained

300g fresh or frozen broad beans

100g dried apricots, halved

1 cauliflower, broken into florets

1 tablespoon flaked almonds, to serve

MY STORECUPBOARD RAS-EL-HANOUT

$\frac{1}{2}$ tablespoon fennel seeds

large pinch of chilli flakes

$\frac{1}{2}$ tablespoon cumin seeds

1 teaspoon coriander seeds

3cm cinnamon stick

1 teaspoon ground ginger

$\frac{1}{2}$ tablespoon paprika

Okay, we've got to work quickly if we are going to get this done in 25 minutes. Pour 100ml of the olive oil into a pan and fry the sweet potato, new potatoes, peppers, onion and garlic until they are beginning to colour.

While this is going on, prepare the spice mix. Grind the fennel seeds, chilli flakes, cumin seeds, coriander seeds and cinnamon in a pestle and mortar and mix with the ginger and paprika.

Add the spice mix to the pan. Tip in the chopped tomatoes and pour in up to 600ml water, add the salt and bring to a simmer. Chuck in the olives, chickpeas, broad beans and apricots and simmer until the potatoes are soft, about 10–12 minutes.

Meanwhile, whizz the cauliflower to a fine crumb in a blender or food-processor until it cunningly resembles couscous. Steam the cauliflower in a sieve or colander over a pan of boiling water for 5 minutes. (A word on the cauliflower couscous... I wish I had invented this quirky yet clever vegetable accompaniment, but sadly I didn't. I stole it. A few years ago I went to El Bulli in Spain and one of the dishes included cauliflower whizzed up and served as couscous. Simple. But ingenious.)

Stir the remaining olive oil into the tagine, sprinkle with the almonds and serve with the cauliflower couscous.

If I were to go to a dinner party and be served *just* a bowl of soup, I would probably take the host to one side and deliver a two-minute lecture on menu planning. That said, if I visited the same friend on a Saturday lunchtime and was served a good hearty soup with lots of flavour and crusty bread, I would slap the host on the back and proclaim them a culinary genius. It just goes to show what difference a few hours can make to a cook's reputation!

This is more than just a soup – it's a hearty main course perfect for a weekend brunch (or any other day for that matter!). The trick with this soup is to balance the smooth creamy flavour of the butternut and the coconut milk with the punch of the spice. I tend to use the word chowder to indicate a soup with texture – feel free to blend it as smooth as you wish, but I think the texture allows the individual flavours to shine through.

Butternut chowder with coconut, chilli & coriander

SERVES 8 HUNGRY PEOPLE

2 teaspoons cumin seeds

2 teaspoons fennel seeds

1 teaspoon chilli flakes

1 teaspoon medium curry powder

800g butternut squash, peeled, seeded and diced

vegetable oil, for frying

4 garlic cloves, chopped

600ml water

750ml coconut milk

2 red bird's eye chillies

small bunch of basil

small bunch of coriander

juice of 1 lime

salt and pepper

Combine the cumin seeds, fennel seeds, chilli flakes and curry powder in a large bowl. Add the butternut squash and toss to coat.

Heat the oil in a frying pan and fry the spice-coated butternut, in batches if necessary, until pale golden-brown in colour. The point here is to caramelise but not cook it. This caramelisation will add another layer of flavour to the finished soup.

Tip the butternut into a large pan and chuck in the garlic. Pour over the water and coconut milk and bring to a simmer. Cook for 15 minutes or until the butternut is soft and cooked through.

Whizz the soup in a blender or food-processor, in batches if necessary, or use a hand-held stick blender. Blitz until fairly smooth but still with a little texture. If not serving immediately, cool the soup and chill in the fridge or freeze until required.

To serve, bash the bird's eye chillies, basil and coriander to a pulp in a pestle and mortar and stir into the chowder. Squeeze over the lime juice and season to taste. Serve with plenty of crusty bread.

❝ This vaguely Thai-style curry is one of my favourite quick and easy dishes. The choice of fish is very much up to you – pick something that suits your pocket and tickles your fancy. The last time I made this I used whole gutted bream and cut it straight through the body and backbone into chunks. If you prefer your fish boneless, buy fillets, but in this style of dish they may break up a little. ❞

A quick spicy fish curry

SERVES 4

2 x 500g sea bream, scaled, gutted
    and heads removed

1½ tablespoons vegetable oil

3 shallots, sliced into rings

1 garlic clove, finely chopped

50g fresh ginger, peeled and grated

2 teaspoons hot curry powder

2 x 400ml cans coconut milk

½ teaspoon salt

2 lemongrass stalks

6 kaffir lime leaves

4 heads of bok choi, halved

1 tablespoon soy sauce, or to taste

3 teaspoons fish sauce, or to taste

1 bunch of basil

juice of 1 lime

Cut the bream through the bone into chunks and set aside.

Heat the oil in a pan over a low to medium heat and fry the shallots, garlic and ginger until slightly softened. Add the curry powder and stir, then pour in the coconut milk, add the salt and bring to a simmer.

Meanwhile, bash the lemongrass and lime leaves in a pestle and mortar until the lemongrass is bruised and frayed.

Chuck the lemongrass and lime leaves into the pan and simmer gently for 10 minutes. Add the bream, ensuring that the liquid covers the fish – if not, add a splash of water. Bring back to a simmer and cook very gently for 10 minutes. Add the bok choi, ensuring it is submerged, and cook for a further 5 minutes or until the bream is cooked through.

Add the soy and fish sauce. Have a taste and add more if you wish. Just before serving, bash up the basil in a pestle and mortar and stir into the stew. Squeeze in the lime juice and serve with sticky rice.

SUMAC

Sumac is a deep red, fairly granular powder used extensively in North African and Middle Eastern cuisine. I tend to use it more as a condiment rather than adding it during the cooking of a dish. Leave a small bowl on the table and allow people to help themselves. It's great sprinkled over chargrilled meat skewers or used to pep up a braised dish. The flavour is best described as peppery with a bit of a citrus twang.

66 This is the perfect pasta dish. A bit of a modern classic in the pasta world, I'd say. Light, healthy, easy and very tasty. I admit that prawns don't make it the cheapest dish, but it's worth the money. You could substitute the pappardelle with other pasta shapes and sizes, if you like. I buy decent-quality dried pappardelle made in the traditional way using whole eggs. If you'd like to make your own, your pasta dish will taste even better than mine. 99

King prawn pappardelle with chilli, lemon, garlic, basil & parsley

SERVES 4 (ACTUALLY IT MAY EVEN STRETCH TO 5 BECAUSE I ALWAYS COOK MORE THAN THE RECOMMENDED AMOUNT OF 75G OF PASTA PER PERSON. I GO FOR 100G AND WE NEVER HAVE ANY LEFT OVER!)

400g dried pappardelle

150ml best-quality extra-virgin olive oil

20 peeled raw king prawns (save the shells for the Prawn and Coconut Bisque on page 35)

3 chillies, finely chopped

3 garlic cloves, finely chopped

12 basil leaves, torn

10g flat-leaf parsley, coarsely chopped

grated zest of ½ lemon

good pinch of sea salt flakes

freshly ground black pepper

Bring a large pan of water to the boil (I don't add salt or oil when cooking pasta but I've met Italians who do, so it's your call) and cook the pasta according to the packet instructions, carefully loosening the clump of pasta into ribbons using a roasting fork after about a minute. Drain the pasta through, bung it back into the pan and pour over about half of the olive oil. It will last like this, happily, for 10 minutes or so, allowing you to do the next bit.

Heat a little of the remaining oil in a non-stick frying pan over a high heat. Chuck in the prawns and fry hard and fast for about 90 seconds on each side, or until pinkish-red with a roasty look and aroma. Reduce the heat to low and add the rest of the oil, the chillies and garlic. Fizz for 30 seconds, tip into the pan of drained pasta and gently mix through.

Chuck in the basil leaves. Add the parsley, lemon zest and salt and a twist or three of pepper. Serve immediately, perhaps alongside a rocket salad.

By the way, all the Italians I know tell me it's very bad form to put grated Parmesan on seafood pasta (and risottos, too). Whilst not wishing to come across as a heathen, or indeed cause a diplomatic incident, I say if you want cheese, you go ahead and have it.

66 Chermoula is a North African spicy paste or marinade very often, though not exclusively, used in fish dishes. There are hundreds of versions, from Morocco to Algeria to Tunisia, and each one is slightly different but usually involves cumin seeds, garlic, preserved lemon and a herb or two along the way. Although I'm a well-travelled chap, the nearest I've got to North Africa is a greengrocer on Ladbroke Grove, North-west London.

Many years ago, as a budding young chef trying his hand at a bit of telly, I spent a day inside a Moroccan food store, with the owner, making a short film about spices. Towards the end of the day we cooked up a lamb tagine with dates on a camping cooker outside his shop, then jumped on passers-by, forcing them to try the tagine and say nice things down the camera lens. They all obliged, as people minding their own business tend to do when leapt on by a chef and a camera crew. All that is except the owner of the store.

He had sold us the ingredients (at a huge profit!) for the tagine, but when asked to taste it he screwed up his face in obvious disappointment – obligingly all on camera! I was gutted and, sensing this, he beckoned me through the shop to a small kitchen where he was cooking fish *à la chermoula* for his supper. We sat and ate this as he explained, very clearly, that I should never again attempt to cook Moroccan food. So for the miserable old git in Ladbroke Grove who derailed my TV career before it had even started, here is your recipe… in my book (ha ha). I begrudgingly admit it tastes amazing. You won't like the salad – I invented it.

Please don't feel you have to use mackerel if it's not your kind of fish – any would work well, but I think oily mackerel is particularly good with the preserved lemon and paprika. 99

Mackerel chermoula on a roasted butternut salad

SERVES 4

4 very fresh, decent-sized
    mackerel fillets
olive oil, for frying

FOR THE CHERMOULA PASTE

1 teaspoon coriander seeds

1 teaspoon cumin seeds

2 garlic cloves, crushed to a paste

good pinch of saffron

2 tablespoons finely chopped
    flat-leaf parsley

2 tablespoons finely
    chopped fresh coriander

½ teaspoon salt

½ teaspoon paprika

1 small red bird's eye chilli,
    very finely chopped

2 preserved lemons, skin only,
    very finely chopped

2 tablespoons olive oil

FOR THE SALAD

2 tablespoons olive oil

½ butternut squash, peeled and diced

handful of rocket leaves

8 cherry tomatoes, cut in wedges

4 spring onions, finely sliced on
    an angle

seeds from ½ pomegranate

splash of balsamic vinegar

To make the chermoula paste, heat a frying pan and dry-fry the coriander seeds and cumin seeds. Leave to cool, then grind to a powder in a pestle and mortar. Tip into a bowl.

Add the garlic, saffron, parsley, fresh coriander, salt, paprika, chilli and preserved lemon. Stir well, then mix in the olive oil.

Spoon half of the chermoula paste into a dish and lay the mackerel fillets on top. Spoon the remaining paste over the top to cover the fish. Leave to marinate for 15 minutes.

To make the salad, heat the oil in a frying pan over a medium-high heat, tip in the butternut and cook until golden brown and cooked through (5–6 minutes). Transfer to a bowl and add the rocket, tomatoes and spring onions. Using a spoon, dig out the pomegranate seeds from the skin and tip into the salad. Add a splash of balsamic vinegar and arrange onto four serving plates.

When you're ready to cook the fish, heat the oil in a non-stick frying pan over a high heat. Place the mackerel fillets, skin-side down, into the pan and cook for 3–4 minutes or until the skin has coloured. Flip the mackerel over and cook for a further 3–4 minutes or until the fish is cooked through.

Toward the end of the cooking time, tip any remaining chermoula into the frying pan with the mackerel and spoon it over the fish when you serve up.

Place the mackerel fillets on top of the salad and serve.

> 66 This recipe won't win any awards for authenticity or creative genius, but I think it's worthy of inclusion in this chapter simply because it's a very basic, quick and simple curry base which can be frozen and used as and when curry is required. Just to get you going, I've included a simple recipe below for spicy chicken thighs as a suggestion for using the basic sauce (a free gift from me), but you could also use it with meatballs, diced chicken, fish or chunks of your favourite vegetables. 99

A basic curry sauce for the freezer, which could become ...

MAKES 12 PORTIONS

3 tablespoons vegetable oil

4 onions, very finely diced

8 garlic cloves, finely chopped

80g fresh ginger, peeled and grated

3 tablespoons hot curry powder

2 x 400g cans chopped tomatoes

250ml chicken or vegetable stock

Heat the oil in a pan over a medium heat. Tip in the onions, garlic and ginger and cook for 25 minutes or until caramelised and dark brown in colour, stirring frequently. Don't rush this stage or they will burn – remember: dark brown, not black! If the onions catch, add 1 teaspoon water and stir vigorously to work the caught bits back into the bulk.

Add the curry powder and cook for 5 minutes. Add the tomatoes and cook for a further 10 minutes or until the liquid from the tomatoes has evaporated.

Pour in the stock and bring to a simmer. Cook for a further 10 minutes or until thickened. Cool and freeze in freezer bags or plastic containers until required (I usually divide the sauce into 3 so each batch will serve 4 people).

Below is one meal you could make from your curry base.

...Spicy chicken thighs with chickpeas & coriander

SERVES 4

vegetable oil, for frying

8 chicken thighs or drumsticks

⅓ quantity Basic Curry Sauce, defrosted

400ml can coconut milk or 300ml water

400g can chickpeas, rinsed and drained

good handful of baby spinach

1 tablespoon chopped fresh coriander

Heat the oil in a frying pan over a medium heat and fry the chicken pieces until golden-brown all over.

Meanwhile, tip the Basic Curry Sauce into a pan. Add the coconut milk or water, stir well and bring to a simmer.

Add the chicken pieces to the simmering sauce and cook for 30 minutes, or until cooked through. Add the chickpeas and cook for a further 5 minutes.

Stir in the spinach and coriander and serve with Basmati rice.

I won't blather on about the Queen's coronation, because whenever a version of this dish is published we get the same old history lesson. Suffice to say that this is the perfect summer lunch – spicy, creamy, easy-to-make, it just ticks all the boxes. Serve it as part of a buffet, heap it on top of baked potatoes, dot small spoonfuls onto broken pieces of poppadom as a canapé, or serve it up with crusty baguette and pale ale at a royal celebration. It's your call.

As already acknowledged, this is certainly not the first cookbook to include Coronation Chicken. However, I think a lot of recipes are too sweet and cloying, or they recommend cooking diced chicken breast, meaning that the sauce is never properly incorporated into the chicken. Roasting a whole chicken is definitely the way forward. So I'm giving you my favourite version created by Mrs Merrett (the Elder) of Godalming, Surrey.

Coronation chicken

SERVES 4

1 freshly roasted chicken

vegetable oil, for frying

2 shallots

1 garlic clove

25g grated fresh ginger

2 tomatoes, finely diced

1 tablespoon hot curry powder

3 tablespoons ready-made
    mango chutney

150ml chicken stock

300g mayonnaise

3 tablespoons coconut cream

pinch of salt

1 tablespoon chopped fresh coriander

Let's presume you know how to roast a chicken, and that you've got it cooking right now. It just makes my job easier. When it comes out of the oven, leave it to cool.

Heat the vegetable oil in a pan and chuck in the shallots, garlic and ginger. Fizz away until slightly coloured. Throw in the tomatoes and cook until any liquid has evaporated. Stir in the curry powder and mango chutney.

Pour in the stock, bring to a simmer and cook gently for 10 minutes. For a smooth curry mayonnaise, strain the mixture to remove any bits. I don't bother because I like the texture (yes, yes... and I'm lazy). Leave to cool completely before stirring in the mayonnaise and coconut cream.

Back to the chicken. Remove the meat from the carcass, slicing any large pieces up a little. Spoon over the curry mayonnaise and mix well. Have a taste and season with salt, then just before serving mix through the coriander.

66 A massive family favourite! Everyone loves a tandoori, but most people think that without the classic tandoor oven you can't recreate the flavour – not true! Amaze your friends, stun your neighbours and annoy the local Indian restaurant with your tandoori skills. If you make only one dish out of this book, make this one. I guarantee you will make it over and over again. In case you have yet to see my revolutionary flower Tandoor pot oven, then I should explain that overleaf you will find detailed diagrams, technical drawings and mechanical data, but this recipe can be made conventionally indoors too. 99

Chicken tandoori wrap in flower pot (or not)

SERVES 4

4 skinless chicken supremes

5cm piece of fresh ginger,
   peeled and grated

4 garlic cloves, chopped

2 green chillies, chopped

3 tablespoons roughly
   chopped fresh coriander

½ tablespoon roughly chopped mint

juice of ½ lemon

120g Greek yogurt

1 teaspoon ground coriander

1 teaspoon ground cumin

½ teaspoon chilli powder

1 teaspoon garam masala

¼ teaspoon ground black pepper

vegetable oil, for frying

4 wholemeal roti breads

2 little gem lettuces, finely shredded

1 red onion, sliced

Using a sharp knife, slash each chicken supreme 5 times to create diagonal cuts about 4mm deep (essential for allowing the marinade to really penetrate the chicken). Tip into a large bowl and set aside.

Next up is the marinade. Whizz the ginger, garlic, chillies, fresh coriander, lemon juice, mint and yogurt in a blender or food-processor until smooth. Add the ground coriander, cumin, chilli powder, garam masala and pepper and whizz again to combine. Add to the chicken and mix well to coat the chicken thoroughly, then cover and chill in the fridge for at least an hour – longer would be better (I often do this in the morning and leave it marinating whilst I'm at work, ready for when I get home).

To cook the chicken, heat a good glug of oil in a large, non-stick, heavy-based frying pan over a high heat. Remove any excess marinade from the chicken and cook, in batches if necessary, hard and fast, for 2–3 minutes or until well coloured. Don't be tempted to move the pan around or turn the supremes over during this time as it's really important that the chicken gets the full heat from the pan. Flip the chicken over and cook the 'B' side until cooked through.

Warm the roti in a griddle pan and lay flat on the deck (the roti, not you). Slice the chicken and arrange in the centres of the roti. Add the lettuce and red onion, roll up and eat!

A tandoor is a clay oven used for cooking meat and baking bread. Its origins are thought to be Indian, but tandoors are now widely used throughout Asian cookery. Nowadays high-tech commercial versions are popular, but in its most basic form, a tandoor really amounts to a simple clay pot in which charcoal is burned. The idea is that the food is exposed to the fire itself, thus taking on a fantastic charred flavour and appearance. It's a characteristic virtually impossible to achieve with our conventional home ovens. My local Indian restaurateur informs me that any dish which is cooked in this way and called 'tandoori' is always a big seller.

A quick squizz on the internet will result in you finding lots of tandoor ovens available to purchase for home use, but none of them is cheap, so I've invented a beginner's model to get you started. This seemingly simple oven represents a major achievement in my life. Believe me, I have a nerve trying to teach anybody to build anything. In the 'man-who-makes-stuff' department, I am a crushing disappointment.

In life there appear to be two distinct categories of men. There are the real men who make stuff – cupboards, kitchen units, garden sheds or tree houses for their children. This type of man paints his own house, can easily change the wheel on his family car and would even climb a ladder to mend a leaking roof. And then there are the men who invest in a nation's economy by paying (cash-in-hand, if possible) a semi-professional local man from the former group to carry out these jobs on their behalf.

Rarely does a man from one group join the other, but I have achieved this with my homemade tandoor oven.

Anyway, enough of this self-help bravado rubbish. Let's get your oven up and running. I've written the following DIY instructions like a recipe, just so that we can all understand and follow them more easily!

Make your very own tandoor oven

KIT REQUIRED

1 galvanised dustbin with lid

4 house bricks

drill (borrow this from a friend if, like me, you don't own one)

length of steel pipe (mine was about 30cm long and 3cm in diameter, and I bought it from the only shop in my high street I'd never been in – the hardware shop)

about 60 litres soil

1 very large sturdy clay flowerpot with a hole in the base (mine was about 38cm in diameter at the top, with an 18cm diameter base, and it was about 36cm deep)

a bag of charcoal

fire lighters

a few long metal kebab-type skewers

METHOD

The first job is the trickiest. You need to drill a hole in the centre of the base of the dustbin. My neighbour (an annoyingly capable DIY-er) pointed out that I should put the bin on the bricks before doing this so that I didn't drill straight through the decking he laid in my garden two years ago. The hole needs to be wide enough to allow the pipe to poke through – another reason why the bin needs to stand on bricks.

Hold the pipe in place so that one end pokes 2.5cm or so through the drilled hole. The other end will just reach the hole in the base of the flower pot – this will create a stream of air to feed the fire once we are up and running. Using the soil, backfill the dustbin around the pipe to hold it in position.

When the soil reaches the top of the pipe, place your flower pot in the bin. As a guide, you want the lip of the pot to be at the same height as the top lip of the bin. It's very important that you pack as much soil as firmly around and below the flowerpot as possible.

You now have a large flower pot firmly encased in soil in a galvanised bin. There should be a metal pipe travelling from the base of the flower pot down through the soil and out of the base of the bin. We are nearly there.

Using the charcoal and fire lighter, get a decent-sized fire going within the flower pot. In my experiments I wasn't brave enough with fire size to start with, and as a result I struggled to build up the temperature of the oven. Feed the initial fire with extra coals so that a third of the flower pot is eventually filled with coals that are glowing red with a powdery grey surface.

Place the lid on the bin and allow the temperature to build up.

Back in the kitchen, prepare a trial skewer – chicken with a simple spicy marinade will do. Cook this by standing the end of the skewer into the fire so that the chicken bit is just above the hot coals. Place the lid back on and give it a good 5 minutes, or as long as it takes to cook the meat thoroughly. Eat said chicken and wonder at your achievement. The Chicken Tandoori recipe on page 129 will taste amazing cooked this way.

My own tandoor cooking has since developed. I have twisted and bent an old pastry rack to make a grid, which can sit over the charcoal within the pot, so I can cook small chunks of meat or fish.

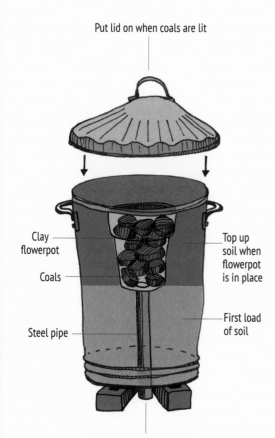

Put lid on when coals are lit

Clay flowerpot

Coals

Steel pipe

Top up soil when flowerpot is in place

First load of soil

Pipe coming through drilled hole

Bhuna is a dish found on many Indian menus. It indicates meat that has been rubbed with spice and dry-fried. The meat cooks in just the juice it yields rather than having a thick sauce added. I'm rather taken with this particular cooking style, and on your behalf I have visited a vast array of Indian restaurants to sample their particular take on the bhuna. Don't thank me – there are worse jobs...

The following recipe is really three or four different recipes that I have finely chopped, whisked well and rolled out as one. Once you have marinated the chicken there are a few options when it comes to actually eating the stuff. Here are three:

1. Toss the warm cooked chicken with mixed leaves, tomato, torn-up naan bread, grilled courgette and red onion and call it lunch.

2. Lay the cooked chicken onto a tortilla wrap with some shredded lettuce, spring onion and avocado. Roll it up and call it a snack.

3. Serve the warm chicken over a heap of Basmati rice perhaps, with a ready-made pickle, and call it supper.

Chicken bhuna

SERVES 4

4 chicken breasts, each cut into
    about 10 strips
vegetable oil, for frying

FOR THE MARINADE

6 tablespoons natural yogurt
juice of 1 lemon
2 garlic cloves, very finely chopped
1 teaspoon ground turmeric
½ tablespoon paprika
4 cardamom pods, seeds only
½ teaspoon salt
½ teaspoon chilli powder
1½ teaspoons ground cumin

TO SERVE

1 teaspoon garam masala
1 tablespoon chopped fresh coriander
1 teaspoon chopped fresh mint

First make the marinade. Spoon the yogurt into a bowl and stir in the remaining marinade ingredients. Add the chicken and stir to coat. Chill and allow to marinate, or... see note below.

Heat a little oil in a non-stick frying pan over a high heat. Allow the pan and oil to get nice and hot. Remove any excess marinade from the chicken and fry, in manageable batches, until caramelised and cooked through – about 6–8 minutes. (The secret here is patience and trust. If you immediately start moving the pan, or the chicken, around you will lose heat from the pan, the chicken won't caramelise and you'll be left with soggy chicken.) Remove the chicken from the pan and keep warm while you cook the remaining batches.

To serve, sprinkle the garam masala, coriander and mint over the chicken and mix to combine. Choose option 1, 2 or 3 from the introduction above and get chomping.

A NOTE ON MARINATING THE CHICKEN

Ideally I would allow the chicken to marinate for about 2 hours. However, having cooked this dish for the last three evenings in a row (to test various recipe nuances), it appears that marinating times can annoy the home cook. My wife, for one, seems to feel that us chefs just write in information about marinating willy-nilly for our own amusement, and that actually it can be overlooked if deemed necessary. As a result we have cooked this bhuna within 5 minutes of mixing the chicken through the yogurt, and we have also left it overnight and cooked it the next day. Both ways tasted fine, which annoyingly means she may be right. Again. So the choice is yours.

❝ In the good old days, serious cookbooks used to employ a quaint system of awarding 'chef's hats' to indicate the technical ability required to make the dish. I have some of these books and I still don't dare attempt the three-hat dishes, just in case I get halfway in and am asked to perform some culinary backflip of which I'm incapable.

I've opted out of employing such a system, but if I had to grade this dish it would only get half a hat – it's that easy.

Bear in mind that, because this meal is supposed to be quick and simple without too much fuss, if you don't have the spices to make my spice rub, start experimenting with your own spice reserves. It's well worth writing down which spices are in the finished mix so that you can make it again if it's a success, or avoid a similar combination if not. Rubs are a great way of using up old jars of spice, and they really can be assembled from any collection of spices. Some assortments work better than others, and if you have a decent cook coming round for dinner, I suggest testing your spice rub first to avoid any mishaps.

Salsas turn up in many dishes across the globe, but particularly those with a Spanish influence. There are some culinary rules to a salsa – they should be sharp/sour through the use of citrus, they should be slightly salty and they should have a spicy kick – but I tend to use the term salsa for a pile of ingredients that I couldn't be bothered to cook! Mix in some lime juice, olive oil and a pinch of salt and call it a salsa. It works for me. ❞

Spice-rubbed chicken with avocado, mango & red onion salsa

SERVES 4

2 tablespoons light olive oil, plus extra for frying

1 garlic clove, crushed to a paste

4 skin-on chicken supremes

pitta bread, to serve

FOR THE SPICE RUB

5 teaspoons ground coriander

7 teaspoons ground cumin

2 teaspoons cracked black pepper

2 teaspoons ground mace

2 teaspoons ground ginger

5 teaspoons cayenne pepper

2 teaspoons table salt

FOR THE SALSA

1 red onion, diced

1 ripe mango, peeled, stoned and diced

1 red pepper, diced

1 avocado, peeled, stoned and diced

20 fresh coriander leaves, shredded

10 mint leaves, shredded

2 tablespoons light olive oil

juice of ½ lime

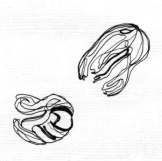

To make the spice rub, simply mix all of the ingredients together and pour into an old jar. Label it 'Paul Merrett's Mighty Fine Spice Rub' and store in a prominent position in your cupboard.

To make the marinade, spoon 3 tablespoons of the spice rub into a large bowl and pour over 2 tablespoons of the oil. Add the garlic, mix to a paste and set aside.

Using a sharp knife, slash each chicken supreme 5 times to create diagonal cuts about 4mm deep (essential for allowing the marinade to really penetrate the chicken). Tip into the bowl with the marinade and rub all over to coat.

Heat a heavy-based frying or griddle pan over a high heat. Pour a little oil onto a piece of kitchen paper and very carefully wipe the inside of the hot pan.

Lay the chicken into the pan, skin-side down, and leave to cook for 4 minutes or until coloured. Flip the chicken over and cook for 4 minutes or until cooked through. Transfer to a plate and set aside to rest.

Meanwhile, make the salsa. Chuck the onion, mango, pepper and avocado into a bowl. Add the coriander and mint, pour in the olive oil, squeeze in the lime juice and mix carefully, ensuring you don't crush the mango or avocado.

Place the chicken onto a serving dish, heap the salsa over the top and serve with pitta bread. For added decadence, offer a dollop of tzatziki too – funnily enough I have a recipe on page 182!

A WORD ON THE MARINADE

There are two basic types of marinade. There is the very wet marinade, into which you plunge meat or fish. The protein is left soaking up the marinade and at some point you remove it, shake off the excess moisture and start the cooking process. This sort of marinade needs time for the soaking and absorption of flavour.

The other type of marinade is one that stays on the meat or fish whilst it cooks, usually in the form of a spice paste. This sort of marinating does not require the time factor as the meat or fish carries the marinade right through the cooking process. This dish uses this type of marinade, so if you're reading this minutes before you need to put a meal on the table you're in luck…well, if you have a spare mango and avocado lying around, that is.

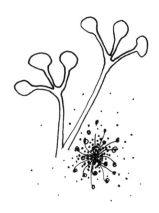

“ Two Tuesdays ago I drank far too much beer in Shepherd's Bush. I was out with a couple of friends, both of whom are chefs, and as we staggered out of the pub at closing time one of them suggested that it would be 'sensible' to head home via the Middle Eastern take-away on Goldhawk Road. I chose a dish called arayes kafta. The next morning I made two solemn pledges – to never ever drink beer again, and to revisit that Middle Eastern take-away and eat the same thing, but this time without the preceding 10 beers. I've kept one of the two pledges – I've been back to the take-away and eaten arayes kafta, which again really hit the spot, but this time I was sober enough to remember exactly what I'd eaten.

So much Middle Eastern cuisine is interwoven and reinterpreted from country to country, but Lebanon appears to get the credit for arayes kafta. Basically it's a toasted sandwich with a spicy meat stuffing. Many recipes ask you to use baharat spice, which you can track down on the internet, but basically baharat is an Arabic spice blend which can be made using spices you may well already have in your cupboard. This makes a great barbecue meal, an easy hot light lunch, or the most incredible dish ever eaten by a drunk bloke in a West London bus stop. ”

Spiced lamb in toasted pitta with tomato & red onion salad

SERVES 4

500g minced lamb
1 onion, very finely chopped
2 garlic cloves, finely chopped
1 teaspoon salt
1 tablespoon chopped flat-leaf parsley
50g pine nuts, toasted and ground
1 teaspoon lemon juice
4 pitta breads
1 tablespoon olive oil

FOR THE BAHARAT SPICE
8 cardamom seeds
1 teaspoon coriander seeds
1 teaspoon cumin seeds
2 cloves
1 teaspoon ground allspice
½ teaspoon ground black pepper
½ teaspoon ground cinnamon
pinch of freshly grated nutmeg
½ teaspoon chilli powder

TO SERVE
tomato wedges
red onion slices
chopped flat-leaf parsley
olive oil
lemon juice

To make the baharat spice, grind the cardamom, coriander and cumin seeds and the cloves to a powder in a pestle and mortar. Tip into a bowl and add the remaining spices. Mix everything up, transfer to a jar and store until needed.

Put the minced lamb into a bowl and add the onion, garlic, salt, 2 teaspoons of the baharat spice, the parsley, pine nuts and lemon juice. Mix well and use your hands to squelch and squeeze everything together.

Slice the pitta breads open and put a decent dollop of the lamb mixture inside each one, flattening the mixture to a thickness of 1–2cm. Close the pittas and push down so that the meat is fully covered by the bread.

Heat a griddle pan over a medium heat and add the oil. Gently fry the pitta sandwiches on both sides until the pitta is nicely toasted and the meat inside is cooked through.

Serve with a simple salad of tomato wedges, red onion and flat-leaf parsley dressed with olive oil and lemon juice.

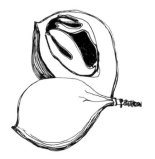

66 Back in my Michelin-star chef days, I would have wept if I had been asked to make a customer a burger. The irony, of course, is that I'm sure I happily ate my share of burgers during those pompous times – I just would never have agreed to cook one!

Nowadays, in my laid-back gastro pub reincarnation, I send out hundreds of them each week! My butcher makes our burgers by hand, using finest Aberdeen Angus beef and they are very popular.

Every now and then we change from the traditional beef burger to this one, its exotic North African inspired cousin, the spicy lamb burger.

You will be keen to point out that tzatziki is traditionally made with cucumber, while I am using courgette. Courgette works well as it has a little less moisture than cucumber, and thus the texture is improved, I think. If, like me, you are a grow-your-own type, you will know that every year you are in for a glut of courgettes, so having one more recipe to use them up is no bad thing.

My Tomato Chilli Jam (page 190) goes perfectly with this burger. 99

Moroccan spiced lamb burger with tomato chilli jam & courgette tzatziki

SERVES 4

500g minced lamb
½ onion, very finely chopped
2 garlic cloves, very finely chopped
1 teaspoon ground cumin
1 teaspoon ground coriander
pinch of salt
½ teaspoon paprika

FOR THE TZATZIKI
2 medium courgettes
about 20 mint leaves, shredded
2 garlic cloves, finely chopped
100g Greek yogurt

TO SERVE
4 floury white baps
Tomato Chilli Jam (see page 190)
lettuce, sliced red onion and sliced
    cheese (optional)

Strictly speaking, one would make the Tomato Chilli Jam first, but we'll kick off with the burger, as it's the 'headline act', so to speak.

Bung the minced lamb, onion, garlic, cumin, coriander, salt and paprika into a bowl and use your hands to mix everything together really well, squishing and squeezing to combine all the flavours. Mould the mixture into four burgers of similar size and chill in the fridge until you are ready to cook.

Next the tzatziki. Grate the courgettes on the coarse side of a box grater. Gently squeeze out any excess moisture and add the mint, garlic and yogurt. Mix well and chill in the fridge until required.

Grill the burgers for about 4 minutes on either side or until cooked to your liking.

Split the baps and toast in a griddle pan to give them a pleasing criss-cross look.

Build each burger with a very decent blob of Tomato Chilli Jam followed by the tzatziki. Feel free to customise your burger with lettuce, red onion and even a slice of cheese, if you wish.

❝ Most French restaurants will at some time offer a steak au poivre on their menu. They often use a prime fillet of beef for this dish, serving with it a punchy peppercorn sauce. As well as the peppercorns, the other feature of a steak 'au poivre' is the addition of cognac. It's never the cheapest menu option! Here I'm using all of the same tricks but bringing the price down through the use of a prime pork chop and a glug of brandy – this is the quick and simple supper section after all! I'm also going to use soft, fresh green peppercorns rather than the dried black version. These can be found in many Asian stores and indeed the occasional supermarket. They are sold clustered on a vine. I would urge you to make the stock using a dark meat-based cube – I would mix it at double the recommended strength. Using a dark stock cube (beef perhaps) will embellish the flavour and will give the finished sauce a nice milky-coffee colour. ❞

Pork chop 'au poivre' with wilted spinach

SERVES 4

4 pork chops – for really decent
    meat look for phrases such as
    'rare breed', 'higher welfare'
    or 'organic'

1 tablespoon vegetable oil

2 large shallots, finely diced

30g picked, fresh green peppercorns,
    lightly crushed in a pestle and mortar

about 4 tablespoons brandy

200ml strong stock

300ml double cream

300g spinach

pinch of salt

The only preparation required for the pork chops is to use the tip of the knife to cut through the fat several times (as shown in the photograph). This will improve the caramelisation of the fat. On no account should you remove the fat – it's the best bit.

Heat the vegetable oil in a large frying pan over a high heat and lay in the pork chops. Don't cram them in the pan as it will lose heat and they won't colour – if your pan is small, perhaps do only 2 at a time. Allow the pork chops to sizzle away for 4–5 minutes and then turn them over for a further 4–5 minutes, by which time they will have caramelised nicely and cooked through but will still be juicy. Before you remove them from the pan, use your tongs to stand them on the fatty side so that the fat caramelises, renders slightly and crisps up. Remove the pork chops from the frying pan and rest.

Next make the sauce in the same pan – don't wipe the pan out. Any residue merely adds to the flavour. If there is no oil left in the pan, add a tiny bit more. Chuck in the shallots and sizzle until lightly coloured. Tip in the crushed green peppercorns and again sizzle for 1 minute. Pour in the brandy and allow it to boil. If you now pull the pan back over the gas ring, your brandy will catch alight, causing an eyebrow-singeing flame to leap up. This has little effect on the finished dish but does look seriously impressive. Pour in the stock, return to a rapid boil and reduce by about half the original volume. Pour in the double cream and boil again for 2 minutes. Turn the heat down to a simmer and allow the creamy sauce to reduce and thicken slightly. Once you're happy with the consistency, the sauce is ready.

Finally cook the spinach. Heat a saucepan over a high heat. Tip in the spinach and let it wilt and soften. The water left on the leaves from washing the spinach is all the moisture it requires to cook. Add the pinch of salt.

Place some spinach on each person's plate. Take the plate of resting pork and put a pork chop on top of the spinach. Pour any juice from the pork plate into the finished sauce and ladle over the pork chops to serve.

" I recently found myself cooking in the Maldives for a couple of weeks. When I say 'found myself', it sounds as though I may have been the victim of the best kidnapping ever... 'Grabbed during the hours of darkness on a cold, grey, wet night in West London, I was bundled into a car by three ladies in grass skirts and bikinis, taken to the airport and flown to a Maldivian island surrounded by white sand, coral reef and crystal blue waters. There I was forced to live in a six-roomed wooden villa on stilts in the sea. Each day I had to cook using only the freshest tropical ingredients including lobsters, crab, tuna, herbs, spices, coconut milk – God, I was relieved when my wife paid the ransom...'

The point of mentioning the Maldives is to tell you how this dish came into being. Woks, griddles, planchas and chargrills were used for most of the cooking, apart from the steaks, especially flown in from Australia, these were cooked on a large, flat, very hot stone. The meat was cooked very quickly on either side and then allowed to rest until just done.

On my days off I was a guest and therefore entitled to eat the steak. The problem was, I was always too full of lobster, crab and king prawns from the chargrill to even contemplate attacking a steak. You are probably beginning to realise how tough an assignment this trip to the Maldives was. I mentioned to my kitchen team that I was having problems getting around to eating the steak so, after service on my last night, the boys cooked up a kitchen feast, and here it is... "

A WORD ON THE HOT STONE

I don't have one of these at home, and I'm guessing you may not either. The next best thing is definitely a heavy-based cast-iron pan or griddle pan, or one of those fancy ceramic plates that heat up in the oven and are then used to sear things (no, I don't have one of those either!).

Smoky beef & green vegetable stir fry

SERVES 4

2 x 200g sirloin, rib-eye or rump steaks

FOR THE MARINADE
3 tablespoons soy sauce
3 tablespoons sweet chilli sauce
1 tablespoon Tabasco
1 tablespoon brown sugar
½ tablespoon fish sauce
juice of ½ lime

The first thing to do is assemble the very simple marinade. Find a bowl big enough to hold the steaks and mix together the soy sauce, sweet chilli sauce, Tabasco, brown sugar, fish sauce and lime juice.

Using a very sharp knife, slash each steak several times to create diagonal cuts no more than 2mm deep (essential for allowing the marinade to really penetrate the meat). Turn over and repeat. Place the meat into the bowl and rub well with the marinade. Leave to marinate whilst you prepare the rest of the ingredients.

MORE INGREDIENTS OVERLEAF ...

CONTINUED... ⟶

Smoky beef & green vegetable stir fry

CONTINUED FROM PAGE 143

vegetable oil, for frying

2 tablespoons sesame oil

1 broccoli head, cut into
    miniature florets

about 20 sugar snap peas,
    sliced on an angle

1 green pepper, thinly sliced

about 10 mangetout, sliced into strips

6 spring onions, cut into long slices
    on an angle

1 little gem lettuce, cut into wedges

20g fresh coriander, chopped

2 green chillies, thinly sliced

4 garlic cloves, finely chopped

2.5cm piece of fresh ginger,
    peeled and grated

15 picked, fresh green peppercorns,
    lightly crushed (available in Asian
    supermarkets; if you can't find
    them, buy a tin of green
    peppercorns in brine)

1 star anise, ground to a powder

sticky rice, to serve

Heat a heavy-based cast-iron or griddle pan over a high heat. Pour a little vegetable oil onto a piece of kitchen paper and very carefully wipe the inside of the hot pan – if it smokes a little, that's great. Lift the steaks from the marinade and allow any excess marinade to drip into the bowl. Retain the marinade. Lay the steaks into the pan, leave exactly where they are for 1 minute, then turn them 45 degrees and cook for a further minute. Flip the steaks over and repeat. They should be charred and dark on the outside and very rare on the inside. Transfer to a plate and leave somewhere warm to rest for about 8 minutes.

Meanwhile, heat a wok over a high heat and add the sesame oil. Swill the oil around and then toss in the broccoli, sugar snaps and pepper. Stir-fry for 2 minutes, then chuck in the mangetout and spring onions. Toss for 1 minute and throw in the lettuce, coriander, green chillies, garlic, ginger, green peppercorns and star anise. Stir-fry for 30 seconds, ensuring everything is well mixed. Dribble a little of the retained marinade into the wok – it should sizzle and sear. Toss with the vegetables, then remove from the heat.

Working quickly, slice the steaks into thin strips and chuck into the wok along with any escaping juice. Tip everything into a bowl, grab the sticky rice and head towards the table.

PEPPERCORNS

You could write a book about pepper... hang on, several people have done (I just checked), so I'll keep this short and cook-like. Black, white and green peppercorns are all berries of a creeping vine. White peppercorns are harvested then soaked and dried to obtain the white seed. Chefs tend to use white peppercorns in their peppermills simply because it's less visible in sauces. Black peppercorns are also dried. My peppermill at home has black peppercorns in it because I prefer the more pungent kick they give. Green peppercorns appear a couple of times in this book. I am lucky to live close to a fabulous spice market where I can buy fresh green peppercorns on the vine. If you don't live near me, you could use a tin of green peppercorns in brine to almost the same effect.

HOW TO MILK A COCONUT

If you came to cook in my restaurant, you would need a pint of water every now and then to counteract the heat in the kitchen. Water in my part of the world is supplied free via a tap, so I'd let you have as much as you wanted. In some parts of the world free clean water is not such a basic provision, and so solutions are required. When I worked in Sri Lanka, the solution was coconuts! There was a cold room with a huge pile of green coconuts. You'd select one, lop off the top, stick a straw in and drink the cold liquid inside, and here's my point – that liquid was not coconut milk. It was coconut water. Coconut milk is made by pouring boiling water over grated coconut flesh. I just wanted to clear that up!

I love coconut milk as a stock for cooking meat, vegetables and seafood. If you were to cook every dish in this book, you would need to purchase a lot of the stuff, so it's worth discussing its availability. Most supermarkets sell coconut milk in cans. These are great and because they're widely available, I've used cans (on your behalf) in my recipe experiments (with complete success, by the way). When buying cans of coconut milk, check to ensure they are unsweetened, as supermarkets also sell that awful sugary coconut milk that barmen like to pour into cocktails.

Coconut milk can be made from dried desiccated coconut, but I don't think the flavour or consistency is great. A much better option is to buy bags of frozen grated coconut to which you can add water, or simply hoof it into whatever you're cooking.

And then there is powdered coconut, to which one adds boiling water. This works much better than desiccated coconut as the flavour is good, and because it's made from a powder you get a better consistency.

Finally a couple of recipes call for coconut cream. Coconut cream is made in exactly the same way as coconut milk, just with much less water. Coconut cream is great for desserts and enriching sauces. Again, avoid the sugary stuff loved by those pesky barmen, and go instead for the natural unsweetened option.

I often struggle to find a suitable finale to a spicy meal. Fruit always works because it's so refreshing, but what if you want to impress? So developing the recipes in this chapter has really been an exercise in self-help!

Sweet, sweet spice

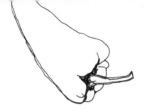

66 Okay, so we all know that panna cotta is an Italian dessert, and we may also know that, in Italy, coconut and lemongrass farming is a cottage industry at best. But I didn't know what else to call this dish, so as it follows the principles of Italian panna cotta production, panna cotta it is!

The pineapple and chilli bit may seem a bit whacky at first, but I'm not the first cook to use this combination in a dessert. Just trust me – it works. You'll note from the photograph that I serve my panna cottas in recycled jam jars, which makes me a modern, planet-friendly type of guy, and also saves a few quid on fancy dishes. I'll let you decide which one was my motivation. A 'soft' dessert like this needs a bit of crunch, so I recommend Orange & Poppy Seed Snaps (see page 172) as the perfect solution. 99

Coconut & lemongrass panna cotta with sweet chilli pineapple

MAKES ENOUGH FOR 6 JAM JARS, THREE-QUARTERS FILLED

15g leaf gelatine

400ml coconut milk

320ml coconut cream

4 lemongrass stalks

100g caster sugar

grated zest and juice of 1 lime

4 tablespoons Greek yogurt

FOR THE SWEET CHILLI PINEAPPLE

200ml pineapple juice

120g caster sugar

1 red chilli, deseeded, membrane removed and very finely diced

½ pineapple, cut into 1cm cubes

Lay the gelatine leaves flat in a tray or on a plate and cover them with cold water. Leave to soak until they turn jelly-like in consistency. Set aside.

Pour the coconut milk and coconut cream into a pan. Bash the lemongrass, a stalk at a time, using a rolling pin until it splinters into shards. Add to the pan and push below the surface of the liquid. Add the sugar and lime zest and juice and heat to a simmer. Cook for 3 minutes, remove from the heat and leave to stand for 5 minutes.

Pass the mixture through a fine sieve, making sure you push through all the liquid. Discard the bits in the sieve. You now have a coconut-flavoured liquid, lightly sweetened and infused with lime and lemongrass.

Squeeze the water from the gelatine and add to the hot liquid. Stir until the gelatine dissolves. Allow the mixture to cool a little and then gently whisk in the yogurt. Pour into 6 jam jars and chill in the fridge for 2 hours or until set.

Remove the panna cotta from the fridge about an hour before serving to allow to soften very slightly. Also, the flavour is better if they are not eaten straight from the fridge.

Meanwhile, make the sweet chilli pineapple. Pour the pineapple juice into a small pan and stir in the sugar. Heat to a simmer and cook until reduced by a third to form an intense pineapple syrup. Remove from the heat and stir in the chilli and pineapple. Chill in the fridge until required.

Spoon the chilli pineapple over the coconut panna cotta, adding a little of the pineapple syrup as well.

66 At first glance, this dessert may look a little complicated, but ignore all the fancy-pants stuff around the outside – I will give you all the details for that in the recipe, but the main bit of the dish is the creamy, frozen semi-freddo under the glazed fig.

A semi-freddo is a rustic-style Italian ice cream, which is perfect for making at home because all you need is a freezer rather than an expensive ice-cream machine.

I have flavoured the semi-freddo with two very pungent spices – cardamom and star anise – which go well with the honey, giving the dessert a Middle Eastern feel. Fig is the ideal fruit for this, although you could use poached plums or blackberries if figs aren't your thing.

Once you've mastered this recipe, you will be free to wander unaccompanied in the land of semi-freddos, creating whatever combinations you wish by using the basic mixture and adding your chosen flavourings. Semi-freddo is often made in a terrine mould and cut at the table. I prefer to use individual metal rings, but the choice is yours. I suggest making semi-freddo at least a day before you need it so that it has time to freeze and set. You could, of course, make it days before and leave it in the freezer. If you're feeling really adventurous, or you need to impress your dinner guests, make the basil syrup too. The flavour and colour are stunning and it goes so well with this dessert, but the semi-freddo still tastes great without it. 99

Honey, cardamom & star anise semi-freddo with roasted fig sauce & basil syrup

MAKES ENOUGH TO FILL 8 X 8CM RINGS

2 green cardamom pods

1 star anise

1 free-range egg, plus 4 yolks

100g clear honey

300ml double cream

The first job is to grind the spices – without a doubt, this is best done minutes before using them so that their full, fresh pungency goes into the dessert. Grind the cardamom pods using a pestle and mortar. Give each a thud and you will see the pods splits open. Inside the green husks are some shiny, black seeds. Separate the seeds and discard the husks. Now add the star anise to the cardamom seeds and grind everything to a really fine powder.

To make the sabayon (see page 152) , put the eggs, egg yolks, honey and ground spices into a bowl set over a pan of simmering water and whisk for 5–6 minutes or until the mixture is pale, thick and creamy (a steady whisking which incorporates all the mixture is much more effective than mad, crazy whisking which renders you exhausted after 2 minutes!).

MORE INGREDIENTS OVERLEAF …

CONTINUED… ⟶

Honey, cardamom & star anise semi-freddo with roasted fig sauce & basil syrup

CONTINUED FROM PAGE 151

FOR THE FIG SAUCE

3 figs

1 tablespoon caster sugar

3 tablespoons water

FOR THE BASIL SYRUP

100ml water

100g caster sugar

small bunch of basil

FOR THE GLAZED FIGS

8 figs

icing sugar, for dusting

TO SERVE

honey

8 teaspoons pine nuts (1 teaspoon
    for each person)

Remove the bowl and continue whisking for around 5 minutes or until the mixture cools. Whip the cream until thickened but still loose enough that it will just about pour. Add the cream to the sabayon and carefully fold in.

Place 8 x 8cm metal rings onto a lined baking tray. Spoon the mixture into the rings and carefully slide the tray into the freezer for 4 hours. Don't touch until you're ready to serve.

Now for the other bits ...

To make the fig sauce, halve the figs, scrape out the flesh and roughly chop. Tip into a pan with the sugar and water. Heat to a simmer and cook for 5 minutes, then blend to a smooth sauce using a stick blender.

To make the basil syrup, heat the water and sugar to a simmer and cook for 5 minutes. Meanwhile, whizz the basil in a blender or food-processor. Pour the hot, simmering water and sugar syrup on to the basil whilst the motor is at full speed and whizz until the basil is completely liquidised. Strain to remove any bits and chill in the fridge until required.

The fig on top to serve is very easy. Halve the figs, dust the cut faces with icing sugar and place under a hot grill or use a blowtorch to glaze (the figs don't need to be warm, so you can do this an hour or two in advance). Toast the pine nuts in the oven or a hot pan until golden brown.

Push the semi-freddos out of the rings on to serving plates and place the glazed fig halves on top. Drizzle with a little honey, spoon around the fig sauce and basil syrup and top with a few toasted pine nuts.

A WORD ON PASTRY JARGON

1. The process used to make the semi-freddo has a fancy French name – you're making a *sabayon* from the eggs, the heat and the air that you're incorporating via the whisk. Expect the mixture to become pale in colour, thick and viscous. Bear in mind that if you neglect any area of the bowl, the egg in that part will cook firm from the heat of the bowl – your mission is to avoid this happening.

2. Chefs often tell people to 'fold carefully'. What we mean is to gently turn two whisked, aerated mixtures together so that the air is retained within, rather than knocking it out by vigorously stirring.

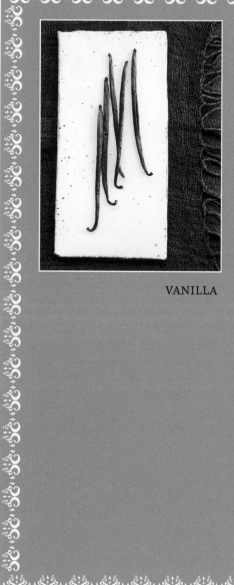

VANILLA

Because of my childhood introduction to vanilla via ice cream, I grew up thinking vanilla basically meant plain, as in no added flavour. How wrong was that? Vanilla is a big hitter in the flavour stakes. If you are ever lucky enough to visit a spice garden, you will be amazed to see vanilla growing on a vine from which long, green pods hang. If you are thinking of purchasing vanilla for one of the many (delightful, inspired and tasty) recipes in this book, here are a couple of pointers.

Fresh vanilla is definitely the best. Well, I say fresh – it's actually steamed and fermented over several weeks before the cook lays hands upon it, but it's the real thing. The vanilla pod should be split and the seeds within scraped out, but wherever possible use both the pod and the scraped seeds because combined they impart the full flavour of vanilla. The flavour is also enhanced by being added to a fatty liquid such as cream, butter or milk, hence why it works so well in custards and ice creams.

Then there is vanilla extract. Not as good as the real thing, but useable nonetheless, and easy to use, too, as it arrives in a bottle. Finally comes the villain of the piece, vanilla essence. This really isn't anywhere near as good as either of the aforementioned vanillas – go without whilst you save up to treat yourself to the real thing!

By the way, scraped vanilla pods that haven't been cooked can be stored in a jar of sugar. The sugar will absorb much of the flavour.

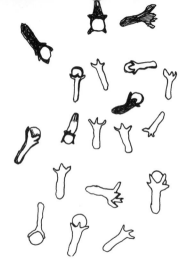

> If my mum comes across this recipe, she will very probably threaten me with legal action, claiming that I've ripped off her famous banana and sour cream dessert without prior agreement. Mrs Merrett does indeed make a very good banana and sour cream dessert, but I think I've taken the dish to new heights with my customisation. The talking point in her dish is undoubtedly the melted caramel sugar topping, which I've kept here. But seriously Mum, mango and pineapple are so much more exciting than the overripe bananas you use, and everyone likes Greek yogurt more than sour cream.
>
> The rice pudding is an element of the dish rather than the main focus, so don't be tempted to cook too much rice. I always use Carolina pudding rice for this because it's the standard rice recommended for a sweet rice pudding, but we recently forgot to order said rice at the restaurant and so my man on the pastry used risotto rice with equally good results. I recommend assembling this dessert about 3 hours before serving.

Coconut rice pudding, fresh mango & pineapple with spiced brown sugar yogurt

SERVES 4

30g butter

25g caster or vanilla sugar
   (see page 153)

2 green cardamom pods

2 cloves

pinch of ground ginger

80g Carolina (see note in intro)
   or carnaroli rice

400ml can coconut milk

100ml water

160ml coconut cream

FOR THE SPICED BROWN SUGAR

100g soft dark brown sugar

½ teaspoon mixed ground spice

½ teaspoon ground cinnamon

TO SERVE

1 ripe mango, peeled, stoned and
   cut into 5mm cubes

chunk of ripe sweet pineapple,
   cut into 5mm cubes

80g Greek yogurt

Melt the butter in a small pan over a low heat. Add the sugar and chuck in the cardamom, cloves and ginger. Let everything fizzle for a few seconds (I should explain that in my book – literally – fizzle happens at a lower heat than sizzle!). Add the rice and fizzle again for 1 minute.

Whisk together the coconut milk and the water (this will help the rice to absorb the liquid). Pour about 100ml of the thinned coconut milk into the rice and stir to a simmer. Add the remaining thinned coconut milk a little at a time, bringing each addition to a simmer before adding more, stirring occasionally. By the time you've used up all the thinned coconut milk, the rice should be soft and edible with a coconut flavour and a little spicy zing. Remove from the heat and leave to cool for 10 minutes.

Stir in the coconut cream and leave to cool completely. Remove the cardamom pods and cloves, which should be fairly easy to find in the white rice pudding.

Meanwhile, stir together the ingredients for the spiced brown sugar.

About 3 hours ahead of serving, evenly distribute the mango amongst four jars or serving bowls. Spoon a layer of rice pudding over the mango, then add the pineapple and top with the yogurt. Sprinkle over the spiced brown sugar and cover (either with jam jar lids lids or clingfilm) and leave in the fridge for 2 hours. The sugar will 'melt' into the yogurt to make a lovely caramel topping … and annoy my mum.

❝ A short while ago, I received a phone call whilst at work. I didn't recognise the number, so I answered with an irritable snarl, presuming it would be one of those dodgy calls from a call centre, trying to sell me something I didn't need.

'Is that Mr Paul Merrett?'

'Possibly... who is this? I'm extremely busy at the moment.'

'Oh, I am sorry. I represent a five-star luxury resort in the Maldives and we were wondering if you would consider coming out here, free of charge, with your family, as part of our guest chef promotion... I could call back.'

'Err no, actually I'm no longer busy in any way... I'll have to consider it, obviously.'

I turned away, covered the mouthpiece and punched the air.

'Right, I've considered it – we're coming. Name the date.'

And so this dessert was born...

You don't have to eat it on a tropical island surrounded by powdery white sand and coral reef, though frankly it will taste a lot better if you do (as with every other recipe in this book!). A glance at the photo may put you off making it initially as it looks quite fancy, but I assure you it is not very tricky at all.

The almond sponge paste, called frangipane by us catering types, is a classic French preparation used in many desserts. I tend to make more than I need and then freeze the excess in lumps for later use. As far as puff pastry is concerned, you could make it from scratch... but life is too short. Just buy a decent ready-made brand.

And so to the ice cream. Ten minutes ago I posted a message on Twitter asking if I could presume that my future book readers would own an ice-cream machine. The answer was a unanimous no. So here's plan B – a trick I've tried at home, after seeing a much better chef than me do it on telly. ❞

Mango & almond tarts with yogurt & black pepper ice cream

MAKES 4 INDIVIDUAL TARTS

300g ready-made puff pastry
flour, for dusting
2–3 just ripe mangoes

FOR THE ALMOND SPONGE PASTE
125g butter
125g ground almonds
125g icing sugar, sifted
75g flour, sifted
3 small eggs

To make the almond sponge paste, beat the butter using a hand-held electric whisk or an electric mixer for about 5 minutes, or until pale and fluffy (if you are mixing by hand, this will take considerably longer). Tip in the ground almonds, icing sugar and flour and beat for a further 5 minutes to form a dry paste.

Crack the eggs into a bowl and break up with a fork. With the mixer at low speed, gradually add the eggs to the paste, whisking after each addition, until well combined. Chill in the fridge for at least 1 hour before use.

CONTINUED... ⟶

Mango & almond tarts with yogurt & black pepper ice cream

CONTINUED FROM PAGE 157

To prepare the tart cases, cut the puff pastry into 4 even chunks. Dust the work surface with flour and roll out a chunk to a thickness of about 3mm, then cut it into a disc about 12cm across (I use a side plate as a template). Prick the pastry disc with a fork and lay on a baking tray lined with greaseproof paper. Rest the pastry in the fridge and repeat with the remaining 3 chunks.

Cutting the mangoes is the easiest bit of the whole recipe, but the hardest for me to describe. Peel each mango carefully and slice off the 'cheeks' from either side of the stone. Cut into flat, half-moon-shaped slices about 2–3mm thick.

Remove the puff pastry discs from the fridge and spread 2 tablespoons of almond sponge paste on to each one to cover evenly. Place a slice of mango on top of the almond sponge, ensuring the tips of the half moon are at the centre and the outside edge of the disc. Arrange a second mango slice on top of the first to leave around 2mm of the first mango slice still visible. Continue like this until you have gone right the way round.

About 1 hour before serving, preheat the oven to 160°C/gas mark 3 and bake the tarts for 15 minutes or until the undersides are golden brown. The tarts are nicest served at Maldivian room temperature, so set aside to cool a little before serving. Serve with the ice cream.

Yogurt & black pepper ice cream

SERVES 4

4 tablespoons Greek yogurt
1 tablespoon cracked black pepper
500ml vanilla ice cream

This needs to be prepared well in advance.

Mix the yogurt with the black pepper at least an hour ahead of time and chill in the fridge. Also put a metal or glass bowl in the fridge so that it's nice and cold.

Remove the ice cream from its container and place on to a very clean chopping board. Keep the container handy. Quickly cut the ice cream into chunks and throw it into the cold bowl. Add the yogurt to the bowl and cut and mix the yogurt and ice cream together using a tablespoon. The whole operation should only take about 2 minutes.

Squelch the ice cream back into the container and put back in the freezer for at least an hour before serving.

66 I was incredibly lucky to spend time working in Sri Lanka, a country where the cuisine is very much a part of the rich cultural heritage. When I climbed off the plane, I thought a banana was, well, a banana. Back in Blighty, I used to pick up the phone and ask for bananas and think nothing more of it. I soon realised that there are various types. In Sri Lanka, red bananas went in the hotel fruit bowls, the large starchy bananas were used in savoury dishes, and the short, stubby, sweet bananas were for desserts. I have since seen these short, stubby bananas in supermarkets, so if you can get hold of them for this dessert then great, as they are an ideal portion size – if not, I would go with a larger banana and cut it into two portions.

The syrup in which the bananas are poached is a big part of the dish. Be brave with the coffee, cardamom and star anise – they are all very strong when eaten, but here they are simply used to infuse flavour. The bananas should be poached and cooled up to 4 hours in advance. I haven't included a brioche recipe as I'm presuming you're happy to use the ready-made stuff, or you have a good breadmaking book. 99

Poached bananas on toasted brioche with coffee bean, cardamom & star anise syrup

SERVES 4

900ml water

300g caster sugar

15 green cardamom pods,
    lightly crushed

1 cinnamon stick

10 star anise

60g coffee beans

4 short, stubby bananas, sometimes
    called finger bananas

4 slices of brioche

good-quality vanilla ice cream,
    to serve

Pour the water into a pan and add the sugar, cardamom, cinnamon, star anise and coffee beans. Bring to a simmer and cook for 20 minutes or until reduced by about half. Pass the spiced stock through a sieve and discard the spices and coffee beans. Pour back into the pan, return to the heat and bring to a very gentle simmer.

Peel the bananas and drop them into the pan. Poach the bananas for around 3 minutes – they will swell and soften very slightly; the cooking time will depend a little on how ripe they are. Remove the pan from the heat and leave to cool for up to 4 hours.

To serve, pour 8 tablespoons of the banana syrup into a frying pan and bring to the boil (as the syrup boils it will reduce and thicken slightly). Place the bananas into the pan to warm through, turning them to coat with the syrup.

Meanwhile, toast the brioche and place into four serving bowls. Put the warm bananas onto the brioche, top each serving with a ball of ice cream and drizzle over a little of the spiced syrup.

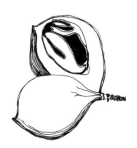

"Tamarind trees grow throughout the tropical regions of the world, and the pods produced by the tree are an essential ingredient in local kitchens. Inside a tamarind pod is a gooey, dark pulp, which surrounds a bean or pip. The pulp is often used as an acidifying agent in dressings, marinades, chutneys, relishes and many other dishes besides. Tamarind comes in various forms. The whole pods, which are used here, can be purchased from Asian supermarkets. Sometimes a tamarind cake is sold, which is basically the pulp, removed and pressed into a lump.

Whilst tamarind is essentially sour, it is sometimes mixed with sugar and made into syrup for use in drinks and desserts. This is one such dessert. The dark, rich taste of the tamarind balances perfectly with the sweet custard. Think Asian-style crème brûlée and you won't be too far off the mark, but instead of a glazed sugar topping this one has a terribly trendy, salted caramel praline crunch. The peanut crunch can be made a day or so in advance, then simply blended on the day. "

Sweet tamarind custard with salted peanut crunch

SERVES 6

200g tamarind pods

200ml whole milk

250ml double cream

2 large eggs, plus 2 yolks

10g caster sugar

½ teaspoon ground cinnamon

freshly grated nutmeg

FOR THE SALTED PEANUT CRUNCH

220g caster sugar

40ml water

125g salted peanuts

large pinch of sea salt flakes

First make the custard. Crack open the tamarind pods and remove the pulp. Soak the pulp in hot water for 10 minutes. Pick out the seeds from the soaked pulp and discard.

Preheat the oven to 125°C/gas mark ½ and line a 25cm square baking tray with greaseproof paper. Bring the milk and cream to a simmer and add the tamarind pulp whilst gently whisking to combine.

Whisk the eggs, egg yolks, sugar and cinnamon together in a bowl. Pour the hot milk and cream over the egg mixture and leave to stand for 10 minutes.

Strain the mixture into a jug, using a spoon to push through any remaining lumps of tamarind. Pour the custard into six ramekins (or you could use a large baking dish). Grate a little nutmeg over each of the custards.

Stand the ramekins in a roasting tray and pour boiling water around the ramekins so that it comes about halfway up the sides. Bake in the oven for 35 minutes or until the custards still have a definite wobble but feel loosely set to the touch. Leave to cool.

To make the salted peanut crunch, put the sugar into a small pan and slowly trickle over the water. Use a spoon to slowly turn the mixture until the sugar has dissolved.

Heat the pan over a medium heat. Don't stir – let the mixture bubble until it forms a rich golden-brown caramel. Add the peanuts, remove from heat and pour on to the lined baking tray. Leave to cool completely.

Break up the (what is now called) praline, add the sea salt and blend to a coarse crumb in a food-processor. (Don't over-blitz – the peanut crunch needs a little texture.) Sprinkle over the custards just before serving.

66 When I was about 14, my mum took us on our very first typical 1970s-style package holiday abroad, to Spain. It left a massive impression on me for three reasons:

1. There were topless women on the beach.

2. My sister and I could electrocute each other by shuffling our feet along the hotel's synthetic carpet.

3. There was a van in the town that sold these long, thin, crispy things that tasted divine.

All these years later I still love topless women…NO, that's wrong…I still love those crispy things which I now know are called churros.

If you've ever made choux pastry, you will notice distinct similarities between its and the churro's preparation. The mixture is dead simple to make and once you've piped out the churros you can freeze them, enabling you to have a crispy churros snack with a café con leche at any time you wish. The churros we had in Spain were doused in either chocolate or caramel sauce, which as a kid I loved, but now I think that makes them far too sweet, and I prefer to serve them with a fruit fool. A fool is a purée of any fruit mixed with crème Anglaise (custard) and yogurt. You can make your own custard if you like, but a good ready-made one is fine too. 99

Crispy sugar-spiced churros with blackberry yogurt fool

MAKES ABOUT 20 CHURROS WHICH, FRANKLY, WILL NOT BE ENOUGH!

300ml water

5 tablespoons vegetable oil, plus 500ml for frying

200g plain flour

good pinch of salt

1 large egg, lightly beaten

200g caster sugar

1 tablespoon ground cinnamon

FOR THE BLACKBERRY YOGURT FOOL

150g blackberries

2 tablespoons caster sugar

100g Greek yogurt

100g cold custard

Pour the water and the 5 tablespoons oil into a large pan and bring to the boil.

Immediately tip in the flour and salt and stir with a wooden spoon for 5 minutes or until the mixture forms a dough that comes away from the edge of the pan cleanly. Don't allow the mixture to catch or it will burn. Transfer the dough to a bowl or the bowl of an electric mixer, if you have one, and leave to cool for about 15 minutes — a good time to make the fool.

For the fool, place the blackberries into a pan with the 2 tablespoons sugar and heat to a simmer. Cook for 3 minutes, then blend to a purée using a hand-held stick blender. Strain to remove any seeds and leave to cool.

Return to the dough. Add the egg to the dough a little at a time, beating well after each addition. (It's easiest to do this using the beater attachment of an electric mixer, but if you do it by hand you will be burning calories, which you can then replace via churros consumption. Every cloud and all that!)

Spoon the dough into a piping bag with a largish, star-shaped nozzle attached, and pipe short sticks about 10cm long onto greaseproof paper. The churros can either be frozen or cooked immediately. Mix the sugar with the cinnamon ready to coat the freshly cooked churros and set aside.

Pour the remaining vegetable oil into a large, heavy-based pan and heat to 180°C. Carefully drop the churros into the oil (you can drop them in on the greaseproof paper if it's easier, as it will come away in the oil). Cook until golden all over, then carefully remove from the oil using a slotted spoon. Drain on kitchen paper and toss in the cinnamon sugar.

Mix in the yogurt and custard with the cooled purée. Serve in a shot glass so the churros can be dipped in.

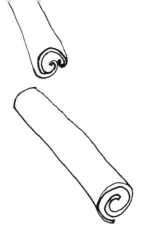

❝ The recipe for Mango & Almond Tart with Yogurt & Black Pepper Ice Cream (see page 157)
includes quantities for making more almond sponge paste than required, and I noted in the introduction that the surplus could be used in other desserts. So, here is one such dessert. I'm including the recipe for the paste here as well, in case you haven't got round to trying my Mango & Almond Tart yet. The paste can be made a day or two in advance and kept in the fridge, or well in advance and frozen until required.

At the restaurant we serve these wantons as part of a bigger, more glamorous dessert, but I think they are great served simply with a ball of ice cream. Wanton wrappers can be bought, usually frozen, from Asian supermarkets. ❞

Almond, cinnamon & cranberry wantons

SERVES 4

40g dried cranberries, soaked in
   hot water for 10 minutes, then
   squeezed dry

½ teaspoon ground cinnamon

8 wanton wrappers, about 9cm square

1 egg, beaten

400ml vegetable oil

icing sugar, for dusting

4 scoops of your favourite vanilla
   ice cream, to serve

FOR THE ALMOND PASTE

125g butter

125g ground almonds

125g icing sugar, sifted

75g flour, sifted

3 small eggs

If you have already made the almond sponge paste, skip this bit. If not, read on. Beat the butter using a hand-held electric whisk or an electric mixer for about 5 minutes or until pale and fluffy (if you are mixing by hand, this will take considerably longer). Tip in the ground almonds, icing sugar and flour and beat for a further 5 minutes to form a dry paste.

Crack the eggs into a bowl and break up with a fork. With the mixer at low speed, gradually add the eggs to the paste, whisking after each addition until well combined. Chill in the fridge for at least 1 hour before use. Weigh 160g of the paste to use for the wantons and freeze the remainder.

To make the wantons, place the almond paste into a bowl and mix in the cranberries and cinnamon. Lay a wanton wrapper on a clean work surface and place a walnut-sized dollop of almond paste in the centre of the wrapper. Lightly brush the edges of the wrapper with the beaten egg. Place a second wrapper over the almond paste and gently flatten it down a bit so that the 2 wrappers meet and the egg 'glues' them together. (I think it's nice if you don't quite match up the wrappers, meaning the second one goes on at a slightly different angle, giving a star-like appearance.) Repeat to make 4 wantons in total. Store in the fridge on greaseproof paper until you are ready to cook.

Pour the oil into a large pan to a depth of at least 10cm and heat to 170°C. Carefully place the wantons in the hot oil and fry for 5 minutes or until golden brown and crispy, turning them over occasionally. Dust with icing sugar and serve with vanilla ice cream.

" Just say we decided to fire a space capsule to Mars filled with things that represented all that's good about Britain and just say I was asked to fill up the capsule, then this dessert is going in, along with a *Monty Python* video, the complete works of Ian Dury, a Brentford FC shirt, a packet of wine gums and an episode of *The Archers*.

Any steamed pudding is worth making, but I think this version, with bananas, crunchy pecans and warm spice, is my favourite. I've included a few serving options because the custard versus ice cream debate rages on in my house. "

Steamed spiced pecan & banana sponge

SERVES 4

175g unsalted butter, diced,
    plus extra for greasing

175g self-raising flour

175g golden caster sugar

3 eggs

3 bananas, overripe browning ones
    from the fruit bowl are ideal

1 teaspoon ground cinnamon

1 teaspoon ground mixed spice

1 teaspoon ground ginger

50ml natural yogurt

40g pecans, roughly chopped

a bucket of maple syrup

TO SERVE (I CAN'T DECIDE WHICH IS
BEST – PERHAPS SERVE ALL OF THEM!)

clotted cream

vanilla ice cream, sprinkled
    with freshly grated nutmeg

dulce de leche (a very decent
    toffee sauce from Argentina)

custard combined with a little syrup
    from a jar of stem ginger

The best thing to make this in is one of those plastic pudding basins. They hold about 1.2 litres, which is ideal for this recipe. Alternatively, use individual-sized pudding basins and reduce the overall cooking time to about an hour.

Put the butter, flour, sugar and eggs in a bowl and beat well until smooth – I use a traditional electric mixer, with the beater attached, but you could do it by hand or use a food processor. Peel the bananas, slice and add to the bowl. Add the spices, yogurt and pecans and beat for a further 2 minutes until well combined.

Spoon the mixture into a greased pudding basin, ensuring the basin isn't more than three-quarters full, allowing space for the sponge to rise. Place a piece of greased foil loosely over the top and secure with string.

Place the basin into a large pan and pour boiling water around the basin so that it comes two-thirds of the way up the sides. Cover with a lid and steam the sponge for 1½ hours or until a metal skewer inserted into the centre comes out clean, adding more boiling water to the pan if necessary.

Carefully turn the pudding out on to a serving plate and drizzle over (drizzle? Who am I trying to kid! Slosh over, more like) plenty of maple syrup and serve with any of the other suggested accompaniments.

A NOTE ON APPLES

Once the apples have been peeled and diced, get cooking straight away. Please don't store peeled apples in water and/or rub them with lemon juice to stop them going brown. These are nasty habits and must be stopped! The apples will soak up water, and that's not helpful, and if we wanted a lemony flavour it would be in the ingredients list. Thank you.

66 This recipe is dedicated to Mrs Page, my first ever cookery teacher, and it is the first dish she ever taught me. I would have been about eight years old and, whilst I had already developed a love of eating, I probably hadn't been let loose in a kitchen before. I still have the blue exercise book in which we wrote the recipes – if I'd known back then that I would steal one for my own cookery book, I might have worked on making my handwriting a little clearer. This isn't the only reason I've included this recipe. It feels like the perfect English pudding, yet many of the ingredients are truly exotic and the flavours tell the story of wealth and empire.

I've changed the recipe very slightly from the rather more austere 1970s version given to me by Mrs Page. I use unsalted butter rather than lard to make the pastry, sultanas in place of raisins and I use a decadent demerara sugar with the apples rather than Surrey County Council standard-issue granulated.

You don't need to wear shorts to make this but I probably did, so it would be a nice touch.

When you've finished your pie, please clean down the work surface and make your way, quietly (no running), to the main hall for a talk on what to do in the event of a nuclear bomb attack. 99

Spiced apple pie

SERVES 4 WITH ENOUGH FOR SECONDS

6 large Bramley apples, peeled and cut into 2cm cubes

75g sultanas

160g demerara sugar

½ teaspoon ground mixed spice

½ teaspoon ground ginger

pinch of grated nutmeg

1 tablespoon ground cinnamon

225g unsalted butter, diced and softened, plus extra for greasing

400g plain flour

225g caster sugar

4 egg yolks, plus 1 white

2 tablespoons milk, plus a little extra for brushing

custard, to serve

The first thing to do is make the filling for the pie. Heat the apples, sultanas, demerara sugar, mixed spice, ginger, nutmeg and cinnamon in a pan until the apples are just softened but not mushy. Transfer the apple mixture to a bowl and leave to cool. If the apples have produced lots of liquid, strain the mixture to prevent the pastry going soggy from excess moisture. It's a shame to waste the apple and spice liquid, so I suggest adding it to your custard before serving.

To make the pastry, place the softened butter into a bowl and sift over the flour. Add the caster sugar, 3 of the egg yolks and the egg white. Mix to form a smooth dough by hand or machine, then wrap in clingfilm and leave to rest in the fridge for 30 minutes.

Preheat the oven to 175°C/gas mark 4. Roll out two-thirds of the pastry to a thickness of about 1cm and use it to line a 25cm greased metal flan ring placed on a greased baking tray. Trim away any excess pastry and fill the centre of the pie with the cooled apple mixture.

Roll out the remaining pastry to make the pie lid. Brush a little milk, or water, around the pie rim and lay the pastry lid over the apples. I like to crimp the edges slightly to make sure the pastry is well sealed.

Mix the remaining egg yolk with the milk and brush all over the pie. Use a fork to scribe a few decorative lines on top, if you so wish, and bake the pie for 30–40 minutes or until the pastry is golden brown. Carefully remove the flan ring, slide the pie on to a plate and serve with lashings of custard.

Compared to our French, Spanish and Italian friends, we Brits are not as steeped in ancient culinary tradition as we would sometimes like to believe. However, there are certain food-related topics which cause great debate.

Years ago I worked on the larder section in Gary Rhodes' restaurant. The larder was the section nearest the phone and it was my job to answer it ('Hello. Kitchen. Paul speaking, how may I help you?'). In one of his books, Gary gave a recipe for Cornish pasties and I can't tell you how many irate Cornish women phoned up to complain about some small detail or another.

Bakewell tart is another case in point. I recently made what I thought was a fairly reasonable Bakewell tart on the telly, only to receive lengthy emails reminding me that the real recipe is a pudding rather than a tart, and unless my family had genetic Bakewell connections extending at least four generations back, I should keep my phoney recipe to myself. Well, I might be in similar trouble here, but I'm prepared to run the risk, rather than deny you what I believe is a truly fabulous dessert. Or is it a cake? Quick, switch phone to silent and turn off the PC.

Parkin cake originates from Yorkshire. Or is it Lancashire? Okay, northern England, and from the several recipes I've tried the main ingredients appear to be oatmeal, treacle and spices. A tip that comes up time and time again is to make your parkin well in advance – if left for 3–4 days the cake develops a sticky richness which, connoisseurs agree, improves the taste.

I'm suggesting here that you serve parkin warm as a dessert, with toffee sauce and clotted cream. However, to avoid controversy I have to admit that traditionally it is served as a cake with a good strong cup of tea.

Parkin with toffee sauce & clotted cream

SERVES 15

350g plain flour

100g self-raising flour

2 teaspoons bicarbonate of soda

4 teaspoons ground ginger

4 teaspoons ground cinnamon

2 teaspoons salt

220g ground oatmeal

350g caster sugar

230g butter

230g treacle

4 tablespoons golden syrup

4 eggs

300ml milk

TO SERVE

450g jar dulce de leche

obscene amounts of clotted cream

Preheat the oven to 175°C/gas mark 4 and grease and line a 24cm square cake tin or deep baking tray. Combine both flours, the bicarbonate of soda, ginger, cinnamon, salt, oatmeal and sugar in a mixing bowl and set aside.

Melt the butter in a small pan and add the treacle and golden syrup. Stir until warmed through, then pour into the bowl of dry ingredients.

Beat together the eggs and milk and pour into the bowl, giving everything a good stir to ensure it's all well mixed. Pour the mixture into the prepared tin and bake in the oven for 1 hour, or until the cake is risen and dark golden brown – a skewer inserted into the centre should come out clean.

Now the tricky bit. Transfer the cake to a wire rack to cool, then to a plastic container, and place in a cupboard for 3–4 days. Ouch! The cupboard needs locking in my house.

To serve, cut a decent portion of parkin per person and warm it slightly either in the microwave or by gently heating in a low oven. Warm a little of the dulce de leche and pour over the parkin. Add a generous dollop of clotted cream and reserve a spot on the sofa to sleep off the joy of parkin.

There will be a few readers somewhat surprised to learn that baklava did not originate in Notting Hill, London, sometime during the 1990s. It is, in fact, a sweet treat with roots stretching as far back as the Ottoman Empire, and has since been a staple sugary hit throughout the Middle East, the eastern Mediterranean and, of course, Westbourne Grove. As a kid I can remember my mum talking about baklava – she had spent part of her youth in Nicosia, Cyprus, where baklava was enjoyed in coffee bars alongside strong bitter coffee.

Back in 1970s Surrey, there weren't that many Middle Eastern confectioners knocking out baklava for the enjoyment of us locals, so my own baklava experience was put on hold until I signed up for my apprenticeship at

The Ritz London. At the time many of the big spenders in London hotels were from the Middle East, so our pastry section made sure that baklava was available alongside the more traditional European biscuits, cakes and desserts.

I like to serve baklava as a dessert rather than as a sweet snack or treat, but this recipe can easily tick both boxes. There are so many baklava recipes in existence that it makes pinpointing an original very difficult, and very slightly pointless because the vast majority taste fabulous anyway!

A quick word on filo pastry – there are many brands available but not all work as well as others, so shop around until you find one that you like.

Pecan & walnut baklava with apricots, Greek yogurt & honey

SERVES 4–6

120g pecans

120g walnuts

1 teaspoon ground cinnamon

1 teaspoon ground mixed spice

3 tablespoons demerara sugar

150g unsalted butter

20 sheets ready-made filo pastry

FOR THE SYRUP

150g caster sugar

1 tablespoon lemon juice

1 tablespoon orange blossom water

125ml water

TO SERVE

200g Greek yogurt

4 very ripe apricots, stoned and cut into wedges

2 tablespoons honey

Before you begin, find a suitable baking tray. The one I use is stainless steel (allowing for good heat transference, so the bottom of the baklava will cook easily), 30 x 22cm and 8cm deep. If yours is slightly smaller or larger, simply cut the filo sheets to fit. Preheat the oven to 170°C/gas mark 3½.

Whizz the nuts in a food-processor until they resemble coarse breadcrumbs, tip into a bowl and mix in the spices and sugar. Set aside.

Melt the butter in the microwave – it wants to be very soft but not split and oily. Brush the bottom of the baking tray with a little of the butter. Cut the filo sheets to the size of the baking tray. You will need 20 layers in total. Once you have cut the filo, keep it in the fridge, on a tray, covered with a cloth.

Lay a sheet of filo on to the baking tray and brush with melted butter. Lay another sheet of filo on top of the first and brush with butter, then repeat with a further 8 sheets to form 10 layers.

Grab your nuts (steady!) and sprinkle them evenly over the top layer of filo. Place a filo sheet on top of the nuts, brush with butter and repeat with the remaining pastry, giving 20 layers of filo in total.

Using a very sharp knife, cut diagonal lines across the pastry almost down to the nut layer. Turn the tray and cut lines diagonal to the first to create a diamond pattern. Bake in the oven for 35 minutes or until golden, puffed up and crispy. Leave to cool.

Meanwhile, make the syrup. Heat all the ingredients in a small pan to a simmer and cook until reduced by a third to form a thickish syrup. Pour the syrup over the baklava into the cuts in the pastry. Leave to stand for at least an hour or overnight, if possible, before attempting to cut the baklava.

To serve, cut the baklava into small slabs and serve with a blob of Greek yogurt, wedges of apricot and a good trickle of honey.

66 I'm including this recipe, a twist on the classic brandy snap, because so many desserts need just a little crunch on the side to wrap them up. I've omitted the word brandy from the title because I've omitted it from the ingredients! I can never taste the brandy in a brandy snap, so why not save the money?

You could make nice, round, flat snaps to serve with a dessert as a thin, crisp biscuit. However, there are those who like to curl up their snaps into various shapes and designs – please feel free to be as artistic as you wish. 99

Orange & poppy seed snaps

MAKES 16 SMALL SNAPS, OR 8 LARGE ONES, OR 4 VERY LARGE ONES, OR 2 ENORMOUS ONES

100g butter

100g caster sugar

4 tablespoons golden syrup

50g plain flour

1 teaspoon ground ginger

1 teaspoon ground cinnamon

1 tablespoon poppy seeds

grated zest of 1 large orange

Heat the butter, sugar and golden syrup in a small pan until melted and gently bubbling.

Stir in the remaining ingredients. Remove the pan from the heat, transfer the mixture to a small bowl and leave to cool completely. At this stage you can chill the mixture in the fridge for later use. If your snaps are not required today, definitely chill the mixture, as they are best fresh.

When you are ready to cook the snaps, preheat the oven to 175°C/gas mark 4. Roll the mixture into balls about the size of a large hazelnut (this will yield 16 round snaps, about 6–7cm across) and place the balls on to a non-stick baking tray, leaving enough space between each one to allow them to spread and flatten out.

Bake in the oven for 5 minutes or until the snaps are a golden caramel colour and lacy in appearance. At this point you could roll them around the handle of a wooden spoon… or allow to cool, then carefully remove the now-brittle snaps from the tray using a palette knife.

> Until very recently, I thought my Granny invented the Easter biscuit. The whole family loved these spicy, buttery biscuits packed with currants, cinnamon, mixed spice and lemon. Being a traditionalist, Granny only ever made these at Easter, refusing our enthusiastic requests for a similar biscuit at any other time of the year. It turns out that Easter biscuits are traditionally cooked and served at the aforementioned religious holiday, but I can honestly say I've never been offered one by anybody, before or since, which is why I emailed my Dad, requesting what I believed to be Granny's very own self-written recipe.
>
> After a lot of old waffle about poor health, bad weather and economic hardship, the old bugger finally dropped the following bombshell:
>
> 'Anyway, here's the recipe – taken from the *Radiation Cookery Book for use with the New World Regulo-Controlled Gas Cookers* (19th Edition, 1936). They don't give the temperatures for Regulo mark 4, but you're the expert and should know. Good old Granny, it's nice that she's remembered, especially in print.'
>
> Good old Granny indeed. The cunning old bird had me believing she invented everything she cooked, and never owned a recipe book! Anyway, family traumas aside, do try these at any time of year. They are fabulous.

Spiced Easter biscuits

MAKES 10 BISCUITS

220g plain flour
110g butter
110g caster sugar
good pinch of grated lemon zest
½ teaspoon baking powder
55g sultanas
½ teaspoon ground mixed spice
½ teaspoon ground cinnamon
1 egg, beaten
icing sugar, for dusting

Preheat the oven to 160°C/gas mark 3. Tip the flour into a bowl and lightly rub in the butter until the mixture resembles fine breadcrumbs. Add the sugar, lemon zest, baking powder, sultanas and spices. Add the egg and gently mix to form a dough.

Roll the dough out to a thickness of about 1cm and cut into discs using a 9cm biscuit cutter. Place the biscuits on to a lined baking tray and bake in the oven for 15 minutes.

Sprinkle with icing sugar as soon as they come out of the oven, leave to cool and serve.

66 Having used my fair share of mangoes, pineapples and bananas in this book, it's now time to use some fruits from closer to home. For a couple of months each year, Britain is the place to be if you are a fruit lover. This recipe makes use of three of my favourites: raspberries, strawberries and blueberries. The mascarpone and vanilla cream works perfectly with the soft fruit and the wafers supply a bit of spicy crunch – the complete dessert, in my opinion. 99

Summer berries, spiced filo wafers & mascarpone & vanilla cream

SERVES 4

100g raspberries
100g blackcurrants
100g strawberries

FOR THE FILO WAFERS
1 pack of ready-made filo pastry
100g butter
4 tablespoons demerara sugar
½ teaspoon ground mixed spice
½ teaspoon ground ginger
1 teaspoon ground cinnamon

FOR THE MASCARPONE & VANILLA CREAM
200g mascarpone
100g Greek yogurt
seeds from 2 vanilla pods
20g icing sugar

FOR THE BERRY SAUCE
200g mixed berries – overripe,
  past-their-best ones are ideal
  for this
40g caster sugar

As with most recipes, this one is easier when broken down into stages.

The filo wafers can be made well in advance – a couple of days, as long as they are stored in an airtight container. All of my previous speeches on filo pastry apply: shop around until you find a brand you like. Whichever brand you choose, filo should always be kept in the fridge when not being worked on. So, preheat your oven to 165°C/gas mark 3, then soften the butter. Line a flat baking tray with silicon paper.

Mix the demerara sugar with the ground spices. Now cut 16 squares of filo to 7 x 7 cm each (this will make 8 wafers – giving each person 2 wafers). Place 14 of the squares in the fridge. Place one of the remaining squares on the baking tray, brush all over with a little butter and sprinkle it liberally with the sugar and spice mix. Then place the second square of filo on top, very slightly offset. Brush the top of this square with butter and sprinkle once more with the sugar and spice mix. This is your wafer – ready for baking. Make another 7 of these with the remaining 14 squares. Just before cooking them, place the palm of your hand on top of each wafer and give them a good press. Place the tray in the oven and bake for 5–6 minutes until they are golden brown all over. Allow them to cool.

The mascarpone and vanilla cream can be made a few hours in advance. Beat the mascarpone, yogurt, vanilla and icing sugar in a bowl with a wooden spoon. Done. Store in the fridge until required.

You can make the berry sauce (called 'coulis' in the restaurant world) fresh each time or prepare a bigger batch and freeze it when berries are plentiful and cheap. Tip the berries (for the sauce) into a small saucepan and sprinkle over the caster sugar. Heat gently until they simmer. Allow them to simmer for 3 minutes and then blend to a sauce in a liquidiser. If the sauce is very thick, add a little water to thin it. Chill the sauce before using.

When you are ready to serve, place a wafer on each person's plate and scroll the mascarpone and vanilla cream on top. Place the second wafer on top of the mascarpone cream and dust with a little icing sugar. Mix the whole raspberries, blackcurrants and strawberries with the berry sauce and spoon over and around the wafers.

This is the section that can turn a decent meal into a fabulous one. Pickles, relishes, jams, vegetable dishes and bread are all great additions to many of the previous dishes and, in fact, some, like Imam Bayildi, Sag Aloo or Matar Paneer, could all count as a meal on their own.

A bit on the side

Most of the savoury recipes in this book would go well with a slab of flatbread. You can, of course, buy flatbreads of various types from supermarkets and they're really quite good quality. If you decide to go down this route, it's worth knowing that all of the varieties will benefit from being reheated in a very hot, ribbed griddle pan, or better still, a charcoal barbecue over the manufacturer's recommendation of a hot oven. But perhaps you bought this book because you're keen on cookery, in which case it's my duty to provide a 'make your own bread' option. Breadmaking is a skill that even some chefs never master. This is borne out by the fact that so many restaurants buy in their bread rather than make their own. Flatbread is an excellent starting point for the novice baker because the process avoids difficult procedures such as shaping loaves and baking at precise temperatures. Once you have made your dough, it's basically good to go.

Flatbread

MAKES ABOUT 12 PIECES

1kg strong white bread flour

850ml very slightly warm water

4 ½ teaspoons dried yeast

5 tablespoons olive oil

5 teaspoons salt

A USEFUL TIP

If all of the above feels like a daunting process to carry out whilst simultaneously having to cook the actual dinner, it's worth pointing out that the raw bread can be frozen. This means you could make it a day or so in advance. If this idea appeals, follow all the instructions up to the point where you have a stack of rolled-out raw flatbreads separated by silicon paper. Bung this stack in the freezer. On the day, take out as many flatbreads as are required and allow to thaw for about 30 minutes, then proceed to the cooking stage.

STAGE 1

One of the reasons people tend to forgo breadmaking is the time involved – this recipe is no different on that score, but with a bit of time management you will be able to work around this issue. The first stage is to activate the yeast. Mix 200g of the flour with 150ml of the warm water and all the dried yeast – mix it up by hand in a mixing bowl. Cover the bowl with clingfilm and leave for 3 hours on your kitchen worktop, in which time the yeast will activate, develop and start to rise. Three hours is a long time, but you don't need to sit and watch it. You could go out for a walk, catch up on some telly or prepare the rest of your meal.

STAGE 2 – WITH A MACHINE

Uncover the bowl. The dough inside will be bubbly in appearance and very slightly risen. Take this sticky dough and transfer it to the bowl of your electric food mixer. Add the rest of the ingredients – the remaining flour and water, the olive oil and the salt. Mix everything with a wooden spoon just to get it started and then attach the dough hook to your machine and start the motor running on a medium speed. The dough hook is designed to work, stretch and pull the dough – bakers would call this process 'kneading'. The dough will seem quite wet, but do not add any more flour. Keep mixing the dough until it comes together as a silky-textured ball of dough – this could take 10 minutes or so.

STAGE 2 – BY HAND

Uncover the bowl. The dough inside will be bubbly in appearance and very slightly risen. Add the rest of the ingredients – the remaining flour and water, the olive oil and the salt. Mix everything with a wooden spoon just to get it started and then roll up your sleeve and, using your hand, work the mixture until it's thoroughly combined. Turn this (very sticky) mixture on to a clean work surface and form it into a ball. In one motion, push the palm

Your flatbread can be flavoured in many ways. Here are a few:

Saffron flatbread – add a pinch of saffron to the water right at the beginning

Herb flatbread – add chopped coriander, parsley or rosemary to the dough at the mixing stage

Seed and spice flatbread – cumin, onion, fennel or sesame seeds can all be added to the dough at the mixing stage

Coconut flatbread – replace 10 per cent of the flour with the same weight of grated coconut and use the water inside the coconut in place of tap water

Wholemeal flatbread – replace 60 per cent of the strong white flour with wholemeal bread flour

of your hand into the dough, pushing it forwards and stretching the dough, then pull back your hand, forming a rough ball once more. Bakers would call this process kneading. The dough will feel very sticky and you will be sorely tempted to add more flour to counteract this. But don't! Persevere ... Eventually, the stickiness will recede and you will be left with a silky-smooth dough. By hand, this kneading process could take half an hour of strenuous work – leaving you plenty of time to ponder why you have never invested in an electric food mixer!

STAGE 3

Put the silky ball of dough into a large, clean bowl and cover the top of the bowl with a clean cloth. Leave this on the side in your kitchen for about an hour, in which time the dough will almost double in size. Bakers call this process 'proving'.

STAGE 4

Uncover the bowl and, using your fist, push the top of the dough gently back into itself in a couple of places. The dough will expel gas and recede in size. Bakers call this process 'knocking back'. Take the knocked-back dough out of the bowl – do this by sliding your hand down the side of the bowl and under the dough and then lifting the whole piece out in one. Place the dough on a clean worktop and gently form it into a ball.

Using a sharp knife cut, the dough into 12–14 even pieces and gently shape each piece into a rough ball shape. Lightly dust the worktop with a little flour and roll out one of the balls until you have a disc that is about 4mm thick. Roll out the remaining balls of dough in the same way. You could stack them up as you go by painting each side of the rolled-out dough with a little olive oil and then putting a piece of silicon paper on top before adding the next piece of rolled-out dough.

COOKING

Your rolled-out stack of flatbread is best stored in the fridge if you're not cooking it immediately. It will be fine for an hour or so. The very best results are achieved over hot coals – a barbecue is excellent for cooking flat bread. If it's midwinter and a barbecue is out of the question, a ribbed griddle pan is the next best thing. Either way, gently brush some olive oil onto the flatbread and lay it on the very hot bars. When it starts to get puffy, turn it over and cook the other side. A little charring is a good thing, adding to the overall flavour. Serve immediately.

66 Baba ghanoush is made from charred aubergines and is popular throughout the Middle East. There are as many recipes for it as there are claims for country of origin. My suggestion is to try several different recipes before coming back to this book and agreeing that the following one is actually the best! It's often served as part of a mezze plate, but I use it as an integral part of various dishes, including my Dhana Jeera Spiced Lamb Rump (see page 96). 99

Baba ghanoush

SERVES 8 AS A DIP

2 aubergines
50ml olive oil
1 tablespoon tahini
2 garlic cloves, mashed to a purée
juice of ¼ lemon
2 tablespoons Greek yogurt
½ teaspoon salt
good twist of pepper

Heat a griddle pan over a high heat until really hot. Prick the aubergines all over with a fork, lay them in the griddle pan and leave to cook for 10 minutes or until blackened. Turn the aubergines over and cook for a further 10 minutes. Turn them on their sides and cook until charred and crispy all over (this may take up to 40 minutes in total). They may smell as if they are burning, but fear not – this is a good thing! The reason for charring the outside is to give the inside a smoky taste. The aubergines will collapse a little as they cook. Transfer to a bowl to cool, reserving any juice.

Cut each aubergine in half and use a spoon to scrape out all the flesh, right down to the charred skin. Place the flesh on a chopping board and chop to a coarse purée using a large knife. Transfer the purée back to the bowl with any reserved juice. Chuck in the remaining ingredients, stir really well and serve.

66 I'm fairly sure most of you will have at least eaten this, if not made it in some form or another. Tzatziki is a great accompaniment to many hot and spicy dishes, so I thought I'd include my version here. Avoid using any yogurt calling itself Greek-style yogurt and instead go for a pot of the traditional strained Greek stuff – it's richer, thicker and creamier. 99

Tzatziki

SERVES 4 AS A STARTER WITH PITTA BREAD, OR 6–8 AS A SIDE DISH

1 large cucumber, peeled, sliced in half lengthways and deseeded
1 teaspoon table salt
2 garlic cloves, finely chopped
squeeze of lemon juice
300g Greek yogurt
1 tablespoon olive oil
½ teaspoon shredded mint leaves
½ teaspoon chopped dill

Grate the cucumber on the coarsest side of your grater – longer slivers are best, so grate it from top to bottom, right along the cucumber's length. Place the cucumber into a bowl, sprinkle over the salt and stir: it will start to release its juice. Hang the cucumber in muslin for about 20 minutes or simply squeeze it inside a clean tea towel to remove as much liquid as possible.

Return the strained cucumber to the bowl, mix in the remaining ingredients and serve immediately.

“ The best mangoes for this job are green mangoes, which are fairly easy to find in Asian food stores; however, a slightly firmer standard mango will suffice. I serve this with Braised Pork Cheeks with Coconut & Lime Leaf (see page 89), but the 'noodles' go equally well with crispy squid or a chargrilled spice-rubbed breast of chicken. I recommend making the pickling liquor 24 hours in advance, if possible, so that the flavours can mingle and develop. The pickling liquor works well with other vegetables, too. Try adding to shredded white cabbage, strips of cucumber or even avocado. ”

Soured mango 'noodles'

SERVES 4

2 tablespoons sesame oil

2 tablespoons white wine vinegar

3 tablespoons fish sauce

juice of 2 limes

25g caster sugar

1 red chilli, finely chopped

30g galangal, peeled and finely grated

2 green mangoes (but normal ripe yellow mangoes would be fine)

1 tablespoon black sesame seeds

Whisk together the sesame oil, white wine vinegar, fish sauce and lime juice. Add the sugar, chilli and galangal and chill in the fridge overnight. This is your pickling liquor.

Prepare and marinate the mangoes about an hour before you wish to serve up. Thinly slice the mango flesh and then shred the slices into noodle-like strips. Add the strips of mango to the pickling liquor and leave to stand for about 15 minutes.

Drain the mango 'noodles' of any excess liquor, stir through the sesame seeds and serve.

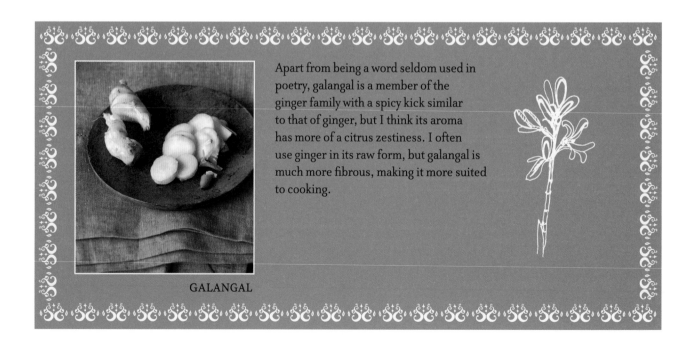

GALANGAL

Apart from being a word seldom used in poetry, galangal is a member of the ginger family with a spicy kick similar to that of ginger, but I think its aroma has more of a citrus zestiness. I often use ginger in its raw form, but galangal is much more fibrous, making it more suited to cooking.

66 Commonly used throughout Asian cooking, crispy shallots can be bought, already fried and crispy, in practically any Asian store, and to be honest most of the time that is exactly what I do. However, for readers living halfway up a mountain or on a desert island, or for the truly committed, here is how it's done. I often serve a bowl on the table for people to sprinkle over their food. 99

Crispy shallots

SERVES 8–10

9 banana shallots
1 litre vegetable oil

Peel the shallots and slice into 4mm rings (I use a mandolin for this but a sharp knife will do the job). Pour the vegetable oil into a deep-fat fryer or a pan large enough to allow for the oil to fizz during cooking. Heat the oil to 145°C and chuck in the shallots. Stir continuously using a slotted spoon for 15 minutes or until the shallots are golden and crispy.

Carefully remove the shallots from the oil using the slotted spoon and lay them on a clean, dry tea-towel. Leave to cool slightly, then fold the tea-towel up and around the shallots and squeeze hard to remove excess oil.

Tip the shallots onto kitchen paper and spread them out to dry further. The above will give you Crispy Shallots but to improve the flavour further try this…

A SWEET AND SALTY CUSTOMISATION — SHALLOT CRUNCH

This variation is used for the Shallot Crunch in the Salmon Sashimi recipe (see page 53). The quantities given here will provide plenty to top the sashimi.

50g Crispy Shallots, bought or homemade
½ teaspoon salt
12g caster sugar
pinch of chilli flakes

Place all of the ingredients into a food-processor and whizz to a fine crumb. Dip your finger in (I tend to stop the blade rotating first!) and have a taste. There should be a good, roasted Crispy Shallot taste as well as a spicy kick and an interesting sweet and salty flavour.

Sambals are big news in Sri Lanka, where all curries are accompanied by a sambal of some variety, and this is my favourite. Serve a bowl of this on the table and let people add as much or as little as they like. My sambal can be served immediately or warmed slightly in the oven first.

Maldive fish flakes are widely used as seasoning in Sri Lanka as well as in the Maldives. They are made from tuna, which has been boiled, smoked and dried to produce a wood-like chunk of fish. Frankly they stink, and when I first encountered them I thought only a crazy person would think that they would enhance food of any type, but I was wrong. They add a depth of flavour that salt alone cannot match. However, if you can't get hold of them, do substitute with salt.

Coconut sambal

SERVES 4

1 coconut, halved

1 teaspoon black peppercorns

1 teaspoon paprika

1½ teaspoons chilli powder

12 curry leaves

1 garlic clove, crushed

½ small red onion, finely chopped

1 tablespoon Maldive fish flakes, or 1 teaspoon salt

juice of 2 limes

Remove the flesh from the coconut halves and grate it using the finest side of a grater. Set the grated flesh aside and discard the shells.

Grind the peppercorns to a fine powder using a pestle and mortar and tip into a small mixing bowl, then add the paprika and chilli powder. Grind the curry leaves, garlic and red onion in the pestle and mortar and add to the bowl with the Maldive fish flakes or salt.

Add the coconut and lime juice and mix thoroughly. Serve to accompany curries.

In his excellent book *The Oxford Companion to Food*, Alan Davidson informs us that the name plantain is given to any variety of banana which is suitable only for cooking. Furthermore he explains that, to the botanist, there is in fact no distinction at all between plantains and regular bananas. That's all well and good if you're a botanist, but we're not. We are cooks, and to you and me there is a huge difference. Bananas are short, bright yellow and eaten raw when ripe, whereas plantains are harvested when under-ripe, whilst still green in fact, are very starchy and therefore require cooking. They can be fried, baked and grilled. I've had them curried in the Maldives, and as a porridge-like dish in East Africa, but we are going to make Plantain Crisps, which are very easy, tasty and a good starting point for the plantain novice.

Plantain crisps

THIS WILL MAKE ENOUGH FOR 4 PEOPLE TO ENJOY AS A SNACK

1 plantain

300ml vegetable oil

good pinch of sea salt flakes

Peel the plantain (this will not be as easy as peeling a banana and you may even resort to using a knife) and cut into 2mm slices using a sharp knife or a snazzy Japanese mandolin. Heat the vegetable oil in a pan until hot, but not smoking hot. Fry the slices in a couple of batches until golden and crispy (2–3 minutes). Carefully remove the crisps using a slotted spoon, drain on kitchen paper and sprinkle with the salt. I like to serve these with drinks before a spicy meal (just feels more apt than Hula Hoops).

66 Every cook has a few recipes that they go back to time and again, and here is one of mine. This pickle tastes amazing – you will love it, I promise. It's worth making a batch as it keeps well in the fridge and goes with so many dishes. I have suggested serving it with Salmon Sashimi (see page 53), but it goes just as well with seared squid, smoked salmon, any grilled fish or as a dip for spring rolls or filo prawns. 99

Asian cucumber pickle

MAKES ABOUT 20 SERVINGS

4 cucumbers, peeled and cut into thirds

150ml vegetable oil

2 garlic cloves, finely chopped

2 red chillies, finely diced

5 tablespoons soy sauce

1½ tablespoons white wine vinegar

30g caster sugar

Grate the cucumbers using the coarsest side of a box grater. Run each cucumber chunk all the way along the grater to produce long, thin slivers until you reach the seeds, then turn the cucumber round and do the other side. Grate each chunk of cucumber until all you're left with are the seeds in the middle, then discard the seeds. Wrap the grated cucumber in a clean tea-towel and squeeze really hard to expel as much moisture as possible. When you think you've got enough out, re-roll it and squeeze again, then set aside.

Heat the vegetable oil in a frying pan and gently fry the garlic and chillies for a minute or so (no browning is required, just a short fizz in the hot oil). Add the soy sauce, vinegar and sugar and bring to a simmer. Add the cucumber and use a fork to loosen the strands within the hot liquid. Work quickly because you don't want to overcook it – 3 minutes max!

Chuck in the spring onions, give everything a very quick stir and remove from the heat. Leave the pickle to cool, then store in a sterilised jar in the fridge for up to 14 days.

66 I love this recipe. It's a reworking of one of my favourite recipes from *Using the Plot* by Paul Merrett (one of my favourite food writers). It could be called chutney or even relish, but jam sounded quite trendy so it got the nod. Eat this on sandwiches with cheese, serve it on the side of a curry or use it to sit on top of the bhajis in Pan-Fried Sea Bass on Sag Aloo (see page 71). 99

Tomato chilli jam

MAKES ENOUGH TO FILL 4 JAM JARS

1.5kg ripe cherry tomatoes, halved

450ml water

300ml white wine vinegar

750g caster sugar

1 tablespoon yellow mustard seeds

1 tablespoon black mustard seeds

3 garlic cloves, finely chopped

2 heaped teaspoons chilli flakes

Tip the cherry tomatoes into a saucepan. Add all the other ingredients to the pan, bring to a simmer and cook for an hour or until the mixture takes on a thin, jammy appearance. Reduce the heat and cook until the jam thickens up a bit more, stirring occasionally to prevent it catching on the bottom.

Switch off the heat under the pan when you're happy with its appearance and carry out a jam test. Place a small spoon of the jam on a cold plate in your fridge. After a few minutes it will set to its final consistency. If you're happy with the consistency, great; if you think it's too thin, return to the heat for a few minutes.

Transfer to sterilised jam jars and store in the fridge for up to 2 months.

66 This simple, sweet relish is easy to make and works really well with the Blackened Chicken on page 80. My recipe will make 1 large jam jar's worth, but I would encourage you to make an extra batch because it works equally well with grilled fish, charcuterie and cheese. 99

Sweet pepper relish

MAKES ENOUGH TO FILL 1 LARGE JAM JAR

1 tablespoon olive oil

½ red onion, finely sliced

2 yellow peppers, finely sliced

2 red peppers, finely sliced

20g pine nuts

20 pitted green olives, each sliced into 3 pieces crossways

50g sultanas

3 tablespoons red wine vinegar

5 tablespoons honey

6 tablespoons water

Heat the olive oil in a saucepan over a high heat and tip in the red onions. Allow them to sizzle away for 1 minute. Add all the peppers and let sizzle for 5–6 minutes – the peppers should begin to soften slightly. Add the pine nuts, olives and sultanas and give it a stir. Pour in the red wine vinegar, honey and the water. Allow all this to simmer rapidly, stirring every now and then, and making sure everything is pushed flat in the pan to benefit from the heat of the liquid. The peppers will by now have softened completely. When the liquid has reduced almost totally, your relish is done – about 8 minutes.

Remove the pan from the heat and cool completely before spooning the relish into a sterilised jam jar. The relish will improve and develop in flavour if left for a couple of days and will last up to 2 weeks if kept tightly closed.

> This is not the kind of jam that one would dollop on top of a scone and eat with clotted cream. No, this is a savoury jam. Well, actually, it's a sweet jam, but intended for savoury food, if you know what I mean. It could just as happily have been christened a pickle, chutney or relish!
>
> As with all jams (and pickles, chutneys and relishes), it's best to bide your time until the key ingredients are going cheap. In this recipe, that would apply to mangoes. At certain times of the year, mangoes can be purchased relatively cheaply by the box. Pounce when you spot them and commence jam production! I suggest making a batch, as it lasts for ages in the fridge.

Mango & red pepper jam

MAKES 1 JAR

splash of vegetable oil

1 red onion, cut into 5mm dice

1 red pepper, cut into 5mm dice

½ teaspoon chilli flakes

175g ready-made mango chutney (shh!)

1 large, ripe mango, peeled and cut into 5mm dice

Heat a small pan, literally wet the bottom with some vegetable oil and quickly fry the onion and pepper for 2 minutes until the onion is translucent but not coloured. Sprinkle in the chilli flakes and add the mango chutney. Stir and heat through, then tip in the mango. Bring to a simmer and cook for 2 minutes, then remove from the heat and allow to cool completely.

Transfer to a sterilised jar, label 'homemade' and keep quiet about the ready-made mango chutney manoeuvre! It should store in the fridge for up to 2 weeks.

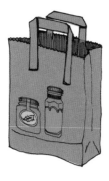

> Most Indian restaurants will plonk a bowl of this on the table if you order poppadoms. It's a tangy dip, which can be made in a large batch and stored at the back of your fridge for a week. It's great with poppadoms, but equally good with samosas, onion bhajis or just in a bowl alongside a curry. I use Greek yogurt because I like my dip to be quite thick and creamy, but by all means use standard natural yogurt for a less creamy version.
>
> The first time I made this dip, I made my own spiced mango purée and mint sauce. It was fine, but somehow lacked the character of the Indian restaurant version I loved so much. A few weeks later we made the same dip at work, to serve with a staff curry. One of the boys decided to cut corners and use a ready-made mango chutney and a trashy jarred mint sauce. Eureka! It was exactly the same as I enjoy at my crafty old local Indian restaurant!

Mint & mango yogurt dip

MAKES 500ML

5 tablespoons of your favourite shop-bought mango chutney

2 tablespoons ready-made mint sauce

400ml Greek yogurt

My favourite jarred mango chutney has large pieces of mango in it (and that's why it's my favourite). If yours does too, you may want to chop the mango up a bit before adding it to the dip. Then all you need to do is mix all the ingredients together and stick it in the fridge until required.

Every year I grow tomatoes in my garden and every year quite a few of them fail to ripen, so this salsa comes to you courtesy of the good old British summer. Green tomatoes have more acidity than red ones, precisely because they are unripe, but that makes them great for this sweet and sharp salsa, which goes perfectly with grilled chicken or fish.

Green tomato salsa

SERVES 4

600g green tomatoes, finely chopped

20 mint leaves, shredded

juice of 2 limes

2–4 green bird's eye chillies, finely chopped

4 spring onions, very finely sliced

3 tablespoons finely shredded fresh coriander

1 tablespoon caster sugar

250ml extra virgin olive oil

Mix all the ingredients together in a small bowl, adding the chillies to taste, and leave to stand at room temperature for 1 hour.

Spoon over a bit of what you fancy.

Hopefully you have all this stuff in your store cupboard, in which case this makes a great, easily assembled dipping sauce for anything vaguely Asian and crispy.

A stupidly simple dip

SERVES ENOUGH FOR 4 WITH THE PRAWN SESAME TOAST (PAGE 55)

4 tablespoons dark soy sauce

½ tablespoon sesame oil

1 tablespoon sweet chilli sauce

2 garlic cloves, very finely chopped

½ teaspoon chilli flakes

Mix it all up and get dipping!

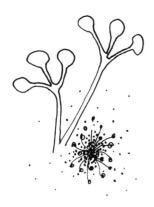

This dish was invented in a West London gastro pub in 1995 and shortly afterwards the UK government passed a law enforcing every gastro pub chef in the country to cook a version of the dish and have it available on their menu at all times... or so it seemed.

Imam Bayildi is actually a Turkish dish, literally meaning 'the imam (priest) fainted', and everyone already knows that fact because, in the late 90s, the UK government passed a second law insisting that every gastro pub chef should, at some time, pitch up on telly cooking said dish.

(Errr, yes, I did cook it on the TV once...)

What I'm suggesting is that Imam Bayildi became a real gastro-pub favourite, but not without good cause. It's a fabulously spicy, evocative dish that can be eaten on its own or as an accompaniment to lamb or chicken. There are as many versions of the recipe as there are gastro pubs in London, and each one claims to be the original and the best. Here is my version, which I think you will find is the original and the best.

Imam bayildi

SERVES 6 AS AN ACCOMPANIMENT

500ml olive oil

2 large aubergines, cut into large dice

1 large onion, finely diced

4 garlic cloves, chopped

1 teaspoon ground cinnamon (definitely best freshly ground from whole sticks)

1 teaspoon cumin seeds, toasted and ground

1 teaspoon ground allspice

1 teaspoon chilli flakes

1 clove, ground

400g tin chopped tomatoes (you can, of course, use fresh tomatoes if you wish – I was just keeping it simple)

2 tablespoons sultanas

large pinch of salt

1 tablespoon chopped mint

2 tablespoons fresh chopped coriander

100g baby spinach leaves

Heat 400ml of the oil to 175°C in a pan large enough to allow for a decent gap between the surface of the oil and the top of the pan (to prevent the hot oil bubbling over). Drop in the aubergine cubes and fry in small, manageable batches until golden brown. Carefully remove the aubergines from the oil using a slotted spoon and drain on kitchen paper. Set aside.

Heat the remaining oil in a flameproof casserole (if you're being thrifty, you can take this from the aubergine frying pan). Add the onion and garlic and fry until golden. Chuck in all of the spices and give everything a good stir. Pour in the tomatoes, stir again and bring to a simmer. Cook until around 90 per cent of the liquid has bubbled away, stirring every now and then to prevent the mixture catching.

Add the sultanas and the salt, stir in the aubergines and leave to cook for 5 minutes.

If you are making this in advance, leave to cool, then chill in the fridge until required. Just before serving, stir in the chopped herbs and baby spinach.

A WORD OF WARNING

If you leave the heat on under the oil while you cook the aubergine it will keep getting hotter and hotter, which could lead to an explosion and your house burning down – and, in a worst-case scenario, this could delay dinner.

66 A fabulous curry featuring green leafy vegetables (sag) and potatoes (aloo).

There are hundreds of variations on this recipe, but I find the one below works consistently well. It can be served on the side of a meat curry, or try stirring in peas, paneer cheese and fried aubergine for a healthy vegetable curry in its own right. Every chef who has ever worked for me will know this recipe off by heart! 99

Sag aloo

SERVES 4

1 tablespoon vegetable oil

2 onions, finely chopped

3 garlic cloves, chopped

50g fresh ginger, peeled and grated

1 teaspoon black mustard seeds

1 teaspoon yellow mustard seeds

¾ teaspoon cumin seeds

½ teaspoon ground turmeric

½ teaspoon chilli powder

1 teaspoon ground ginger

1 teaspoon salt

1kg potatoes, peeled and cut into bite-sized chunks

150g baby spinach leaves

Heat the oil and lightly fry the onion, garlic and ginger until golden brown – this could take 10 minutes or so. Add the spices and salt and fry for a minute, then tip in the potatoes and mix well. Pour over enough water to *almost half-cover* the potatoes – less is better than too much! Bring the water to a simmer, cover the pan and cook until the potatoes are just cooked through.

Remove the pan from the heat and leave the potatoes to cool and absorb more of the excess liquid, which is a good thing. (You could skip this cooling manoeuvre and just stir in the spinach and serve, but I think it's important that the potatoes have time to absorb the cooking liquor so that they are flavoured throughout.)

The finished dish needs to be moist but not too wet, so a little of the cooking liquor may need to be removed prior to reheating. When you are ready to serve, gently reheat the potatoes and stir in the spinach.

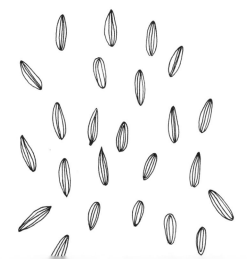

Ready meals have come a long way in recent years, and I'm not ashamed to own up to enjoying a lasagne or fish pie every now and then. However, there are some dishes that have eluded the ready-made brigade. Scotch eggs are always overcooked, cold and disappointing. Battered fried fish is awful, and onion bhajis are not far behind. The thing about an onion bhaji is that it must be made, fried and eaten all within a short space of time. And that can mean only one thing… make your own.

Another option, and what we do at the restaurant, is to shape the uncooked bhaji mixture on to greaseproof paper and cut it into flat discs, using a pastry cutter, on pieces of silicon paper. We then freeze the discs and fry from frozen as required.

Onion bhajis

MAKES 6–8

250g onions, very, very finely sliced

pinch of salt

1 teaspoon ground cumin

1 teaspoon ground coriander

1 teaspoon chilli powder

½ teaspoon ground turmeric

2 cardamom pods, seeds only, ground to a powder

½ teaspoon garam masala

1 tablespoon chopped fresh coriander

5 mint leaves, finely shredded

1 teaspoon rice flour

80g chickpea flour (also known as gram flour or besan – we may not need this much, but have it ready)

vegetable oil, for frying

Put the onions in a large bowl and sprinkle over the salt. Rub the salted onions by hand until they release a little moisture, then add the spices and rub these in too. Add the fresh coriander and mint leaves and mix. Add the rice flour and 40g of the chickpea flour and mix in really well by hand, adding a little of the remaining chickpea flour at a time (you may not need all of it), until the mixture forms a sticky batter. If the onions don't release much moisture, you may need to add a splash of water. I expect you will need to use at least 75% of the suggested weight of chickpea flour, but obviously some onions are juicier than others! You are looking for a batter-like consistency that combines the onions.

Pour the oil into a large pan to a depth of at least 10cm and heat to 175°C. To test the mixture, roll a little into a ball and drop into the oil. Fry until golden brown, drain and eat. If you think it's a little dry or if it breaks up in the oil, add more water to the mixture. If it is too wet to handle, add a little more chickpea flour. Once you are happy with the consistency, roll the mixture into 6–8 bhajis and fry until golden brown. Carefully remove from the oil using a slotted spoon, drain on kitchen paper and serve.

A mixture of Indian spices dependent on the region of origin – masala literally means mixture. Cumin, cinnamon, cloves and coriander are regularly used in garam masala, but so are other spices not beginning with C! As your spice cookery develops you may like to make up your own blends for different curries.

GARAM MASALA

" I have a theory of evolution when it comes to cooking rice. Many, many years ago, someone, somewhere, recorded the very first rice-cooking recipe which suggested using 50–60g raw rice. I don't know who that was, but I do know that they were either on a diet or that they wrote their recipe immediately after a big lunch because, frankly, they grossly underestimated the amount of rice the average person eats. The second person to include a rice-cooking recipe simply didn't bother with research and just copied down the same amount and this kept happening all the way down the line until this very book. Check your packet of rice in the cupboard – I bet it recommends cooking 60g per person. But that's just not enough – not in my house, anyway!

Basmati rice is often thought to be the tricky variety to cook because it's best cooked through absorption of steam rather than in excess boiling water. This means that getting the water level right is crucial. A Bangladeshi kitchen porter at The Ritz London taught me this method and though it may appear quirky, it guarantees perfect rice every time. The banana leaf mentioned in the title is just a neat little trick to keep steaming rice hot. It's not essential but is a nice touch. "

Basmati rice in a banana leaf

DEFINITELY ENOUGH FOR 4

1 tablespoon vegetable oil
1 onion, finely chopped
1 garlic clove, finely chopped
1 star anise
small piece of cinnamon stick
5 cardamom pods
320g Basmati rice

A NOTE ON COOKING RICE

Rice contains starch, and if you rub the grains together you will release that starch. In a risotto this is exactly what is needed, so you stir to release the starch and create a creamy texture. When cooking Basmati rice, you want to avoid releasing the starch or you will end up with a gummy, glue-like mess that will disappoint even your best friend. Always work the rice gently and carefully to avoid breaking or scratching the grains. Lecture over.

Heat the oil in a lidded pan large enough to allow the rice to swell by five or six times its volume as it cooks. Add the onion, garlic, star anise, cinnamon and cardamom pods and fry for 3 minutes until the onion is softened but not coloured.

Meanwhile, pour the rice into a sieve and rinse under the cold tap for a minute. Allow the rice to drain, then add to the pan. Carefully stir using a wooden spoon.

Fill a large jug with cold water (I haven't given a measurement on purpose). Gently pour water into the pan until it just covers the rice. Put your index finger into the pan so the tip of your finger touches the rice, then pour in more water until it reaches the first joint of your finger (this may seem mad, but it works). Now remove your finger!

Bring to the boil, cover the pan with foil and the lid to trap the steam and cook for exactly 5 minutes, then switch off the heat and leave well alone for 20 minutes. Don't be tempted to lift the lid or the steam will escape.

Lift the lid and marvel at this ingenious idea. Lightly fluff up the cooked rice with a fork and serve

THE BANANA LEAF BIT

This isn't an ingredient, more a piece of homemade kitchen equipment that adds a nice finish to your spicy efforts. Cut a disc of banana leaf twice the size of the bowl in which you will serve your rice. Make a cut from the centre of the banana leaf to the edge and fold into a cone. Secure the cone with a cocktail stick and place on top of the rice, thus trapping the escaping steam and keeping the rice nice and hot.

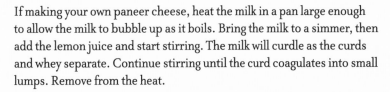 Matar paneer must be one of the most-ordered side dishes in any Indian restaurant, and each establishment seems to have a slightly different take on this simple North Indian curry of peas and cheese. I've included a recipe for making your own paneer because it's so straightforward that it's well worth having a go. However, most supermarkets stock paneer, so feel free to skip that bit if you want an easier life. Whilst this dish is often listed in the side-order section of a menu, there's no reason why it can't be a meal in itself – it really is that good. 🙙🙙

Matar paneer (cheesy peas!)

SERVES 4

vegetable oil, for frying

1 large onion, finely chopped

3 garlic cloves, finely chopped

50g fresh ginger, peeled and grated

1 teaspoon coriander seeds

1 teaspoon cumin seeds

1 teaspoon yellow mustard seeds

½ teaspoon chilli flakes

1 teaspoon ground turmeric

10 curry leaves

400g tin chopped tomatoes

200ml coconut milk

200g peas

FOR THE PANEER CHEESE

2 litres whole milk

4 tablespoons lemon juice

If making your own paneer cheese, heat the milk in a pan large enough to allow the milk to bubble up as it boils. Bring the milk to a simmer, then add the lemon juice and start stirring. The milk will curdle as the curds and whey separate. Continue stirring until the curd coagulates into small lumps. Remove from the heat.

Line a large sieve or colander with a square of muslin or cheesecloth and place it over a bowl. Strain the milk through the muslin and discard the whey.

Lift the cheese, still in the muslin, out of the sieve and give it a gentle squeeze to remove any residual moisture. Wrap the cheese tightly in the muslin, place into a dish and place a heavy weight on top. We use a house brick wrapped in foil.

Leave the weight in place for 40 minutes or until the cheese has condensed into a block. Either remove the cheese from the muslin and use straight away or leave it wrapped in the muslin and chill in the fridge overnight.

And now for the cheesy peas. Heat a splash of oil in a pan over a medium heat and chuck in the onion, garlic and ginger. Fry for a few minutes or until golden brown and softened, stirring every so often.

Meanwhile, grind the coriander seeds, cumin seeds, mustard seeds and chilli flakes to a powder in a pestle and mortar, then add to the pan along with the turmeric and curry leaves and stir well.

Add the tomatoes and cook until the juice has reduced by about half.

Pour in the coconut milk and bring to a simmer, then cook until a thick sauce forms – about 10 minutes.

At this point I tend to try a spot of multi-tasking. Break up 225g of the paneer cheese, heat 1 tablespoon oil in a frying pan and fry the paneer until lightly golden brown. Meanwhile, tip the peas into the curry sauce and allow to simmer. Add the cheese to the peas and serve.

66 I'm including this under pressure from my children as it was their drink of choice last summer.

Once you have made the sugar syrup, store it in the fridge. Then all you need to do is keep a couple of limes (or lemons) in the fruit bowl and you're away. 99

Lime cordial

MAKES 1 LITRE OF SUGAR SYRUP / RECIPE SERVES 4

FOR THE SUGAR SYRUP
1 litre water
400g caster sugar
4 cardamom pods
200g fresh ginger, unpeeled
8 lemongrass stalks

TO SERVE
ice
juice of 3–4 limes
20 mint leaves
still or sparkling water

To make the sugar syrup, pour the water and sugar into a pan and bring to a simmer, stirring occasionally. Bash the cardamom pods, ginger and lemongrass in a pestle and mortar and add to the pan. Continue to cook until reduced by half. Remove from the heat and leave to cool and infuse overnight.

Strain through a very fine sieve or muslin and then decant into a sterilised bottle and store in the fridge for up to 2 weeks.

To serve, put a few ice cubes into four glasses and pour over the lime juice. Rub the mint leaves to bruise and add to the glasses. Fill each glass three-quarters full with still or sparkling water (I like fizzy water, but it's not a deal breaker).

Serve with a small jug of the sugar syrup and let your guests add this to taste.

66 One of the keenest debates in the wine world centres around which wines (if any) go perfectly with spicy food. The Gewürztraminer grape produces an aromatic wine that many feel is the best match, while others prefer beer – Asian beers are very obviously the popular ones to serve with a curry or a bowl of hot Thai noodles. But there are other options, and I've included a couple in this chapter. Both make a darn good drink whether you are eating or not. This cordial works perfectly as a long, cool, non-alcoholic drink, but just to reassure my mother, it also works well with a double vodka shot added to it. Best of all, it's practically free!

Ironically (though I don't know whether they themselves have noted the irony), many of the finest and thus most expensive restaurants in the world have built their gastronomic reputations on (free) wild ingredients, foraged from their local area. Many of the restaurants that currently find themselves listed amongst the World's Best Restaurants go in for the noble pursuit of 'wildculture', which basically amounts to foraging. If you are new to this trendy (yet centuries-old) gastronomic pursuit, I shall give you a very basic starting point so that you too can benefit from a bit of free food.

Elderflower is the blossom found growing on a tree called an elder. Obvious really, but you're a beginner, so I wanted to cover all bases. The blossom is a creamy white colour and is excellent for making cordial, from which you can create sorbets, granitas and jellies, or simply make into a great cold drink on a hot day. Later in the season, the blossom that you didn't pick will form clusters of dark berries – you guessed it, elderberries – which can be used to make jam or fruit pies.

I make industrial quantities of this cordial each season and freeze it in plastic bottles. This recipe is dedicated to the memory of my mate Stella who was the elderflower queen of West London. Every year at the appropriate time I'd get a text telling me where I could find a bounty of blooms. 99

Elderflower & ginger cordial

MAKES ABOUT 2½ LITRES

50 heads of elderflower
2½ litres water
3.5kg caster sugar
3 lemons
300g fresh ginger, unpeeled
75g citric acid

Give the elderflowers the once over to make sure there are no insects in residence, then set aside in a large bowl. You could even wash them if you want, but most foragers are an organic lot who tend to skip this bit.

Pour the water into a large pan, bring to the boil and add the sugar.

Meanwhile, prepare the lemons. Peel 1 of the lemons and discard the peel, then halve all 3 and chuck in with the elderflowers. Bash the ginger to a pulp using a rolling pin, baseball bat or similar implement of destruction, and throw it into the elderflower bowl. Pour the boiling water and sugar over the elderflowers, lemons and ginger and stir in the citric acid. Leave to stand at room temperature overnight.

Strain through a very fine sieve or muslin and then decant into sterilised bottles. All you need now is a fabulous spicy recipe book (hang on … that's lucky) and some cold water to dilute the cordial. The cordial will keep in the freezer for up to 3 months, or in the fridge for up to 1 month.

Index

Acknowledgements

Whilst one who is tasked with writing a book can, at times, feel lonely and isolated, there are, in truth, so many people who contributed in so many different ways...

Huge thanks to MJ, Ellie and Richie for belief and support (and at times ruthless honesty!).

Big thanks, too, are due to my business partner Greg Bellamy and the whole team at The Victoria, especially my kitchen team, Charlie, Damo, Luke, Tom, Eloise, Tomas, Binay, and Will, for covering me when I was busy writing and for their help in developing, testing, retesting and perfecting many of the recipes.

Thanks also to Nigel (the old man) and Coleen Merrett, Ali Guther, Anton Manganaro, Chris Marriott, Dan Pennington, Roger Elliot, Adam Gaunt-Evans, Melanie Jappy and Bernard Zieja for spicy encouragement, inspiration, distraction and support – past and present.

Thanks to 'Team DML', particularly Borra Garson and Jan Croxson, for pushing me into this in the first place.

And last but not least enormous thanks to the finest 'book building' team ever – Kyle Cathie for giving me the chance, my (very patient and understanding) editor Sophie Allen, amazing photographer Jan Baldwin, Queen of props Lesley Dilcock, the world's most talented food stylist Annie Rigg and designer and quirky doodler Anita Mangan.